Mean
Little
deaf
Queer

A MEMOIR

WITH A NEW AFTERWORD

Terry Galloway

Beacon Press
Boston

Beacon Press
Boston, Massachusett
www.beacon.org

Beacon Press books
are published under the auspices of
the Unitarian Universalist Association of Congregations.

28 27 26 25   8 7 6 5 4 3 2 1

This book is printed on acid-free paper
that meets the uncoated paper ANSI/NISO
specifications for permanence as revised in 1992.

Text design by Yvonne Tsang at
Wilsted & Taylor Publishing Services

Library of Congress Cataloging-in-Publication Data

Galloway, Terry.
Mean little deaf queer : a memoir / Terry Galloway.
p. cm.
isbn-13: 978-0-8070-1964-1 (paperback : alk. paper)
1. Galloway, Terry. 2. Deaf women—United States—Biography.
3. Deaf artists—United States—Biography. 4. Lesbians—
United States—Biography I. Title.
HV2534.G3G35 2009
362.4′2092—dc22
[B]   2008036235

For my complex and loving family:
Edna, Paul, Gail (Trudy),
Tenley, Tim, my two nephews,
and my truest of true loves,
Donna Marie.

My sister is persistent.
She wants to get the story straight,
or as straight as she wants it
for her own purposes.

Gail Galloway Adams,
"The Teller's Tale," in
The Purchase of Order: Stories

CONTENTS

Nine

THE YEAR I TURNED NINE, months before anyone knew I was going deaf, the voices of everyone I loved had all but disappeared. Their chatter had been like the nattering of birds in the trees—a cheerful if sometimes annoying reminder of how alive the world was around me. As their voices lapsed away, I no longer felt sure how any but the most common words sounded, how they ought to be pronounced, and that made me uneasy about opening my mouth. My place in the family that year was to watch, which was how I was learning to listen. I'd sit at the kitchen table—where most stories of any importance were told—and read lips, piecing together the shapes they formed until they made a kind of sense. Lip reading—whether you know you're doing it or not—is a hard, intimate business, and during my ninth year, when the way people sucked or licked their teeth as they were talking took sneaking precedence over the look in their eyes, all that rapt staring at mouths would wring me dry. After every couple of stories, I'd turn my gaze away, give myself a breather, and recharge. It took me so much concentrated effort to make sense, much less sentences, out of the lips as they moved, that any and every utterance had to have a payoff. If people were making idle conversation or empty yak about, say, grocery shopping or getting their nails done, I'd heave the sigh of the doomed and lean my head against the table, pressing the bridge of my nose against the metal rim hard enough to dig a furrow. I'd glance up every now and then to see if the topic had changed to something more interesting, like who had died and what had killed them. If talk was stalled at yellow versus white onions or the rising price of a pedicure, I'd get to pitying myself, slaving like a dung beetle over a worthless bit of nothing, and give up—put my head back down on the table, close my eyes, and deliberately lose control. The rising, falling mumble of those incomprehensible voices would wash over me until sounds would inexplicably leap from the muttering to shake themselves clear in my mind as words. A name, the time of night, the make of a car, a part of town, a tired old cliché. I'd string them together as randomly as I caught them, but they still always seemed to be telling me a story. *Ruby, two a.m., Ford, east of Hutto, dying of hunger,* and I'd see the black-eyed Great-Aunt Ruby I'd never met gunning her Mustang down the one main street of a hick Texas town en route to love or a Burger King. It soothed my hurt and anger to imagine all those arbitrary words telling me the illicit secrets behind everything I hadn't heard.

Which may be why I now find myself enamored of the memoir. The good ones thrill me every bit as much as the great novels, but it's the crappy ones I've lost my heart to. They make me feel like a rescue dog, sniffing out the dim glimmerings of feelings sincere and raw within a tangled wreckage of inchoate ramblings and obvious lies. I've been reading a ton of bad ones lately, most of which I've gotten only halfway through. They are piled up by my bedside and not in the best of shape. I'm a passionate reader and the books have suffered for it, their covers wavy from having been dropped in the tub, spines busted from being tossed on the floor, pages folded, creased, coffee-stained, and marked with ink. Red. I feel intensely fond of the whole lot of lousy writing that has found its way to print because I smell in those stinkers a fecund democracy. Every sort of half-coherent loser getting their say. Maybe even mean little deaf queers like me.

As a toddler I was an ardent chatterbox, with such an adult and rapid-fire vocabulary that one of our German neighbors in Stuttgart mistook me for a dwarf. By age seven I was becoming what passes in our family of energetic talkers as taciturn, more like my father, who would sneak away from the kitchen table in the middle of a detailed piece of family gossip my mother and my sister, Trudy, were sharing and flee to the bathroom so he could read the Sunday paper in peace. I never left the table. I just stopped talking. My mother and Trudy never worried about my growing silence—they'd taken it as appreciative. But then they didn't know the reasons behind it. Sounds had started disappearing all around me. I didn't know where to, and I didn't think to ask—not then and not the handful of years later when I started having my "visions." Or so I liked to call them, although they never clued me in to anything useful or remotely prophetic.

Whatever they were, they were first visited upon me when I was nine and our family had resettled from Berlin, Germany, to Fort Hood, Texas. One hot spring Texas night I was sprawled on the dry grass of our new front yard, gazing up at a spiral of stars, when I suddenly found myself six feet in the air, looking down at myself lying on the grass looking up at those stars. I was a little pissed off by how perfectly cheerful my body seemed without me.

These odd displacements weren't exactly a daily occurrence, but that year, they happened often enough to make themselves familiar. Once I went zooming to the ceiling of the school gym as if sucked up by a vacuum. I dangled there looking down on a scene that was small as a dollhouse, everything normal about it. My PE teacher blew herself red on her whistle while my six classmates and I, all of us looking a bit zaftig in our blue shorts and white snap blouses, thundered across the polished wooden floor. No one else seemed aware that while my body was stampeding along with the rest of the herd, I wasn't there at all. I'd become a much more delicate presence adrift in the rafters, smiling down on our sweaty race as if it were a mildly amusing bit of low comedy. Decades later in London, where I'd gone to perform one of my one-woman shows, I saw something of the same kind of life in miniature in a penny-mechanical shop. A carved wooden man, not much bigger than my own thumb, was sleeping on a perfectly detailed cloth and wooden bed inside his tiny bedroom. He slept there until I dropped in a coin that clicked the switch that set it all in motion. With a ticking noise, the window of his minuscule room flew open and a dream horse, its nostrils and eyes painted to look as wild and flaring as its mane, poked its head through the gap. Up the little man sat, his closed doll eyes snapping wide with alarm as the horse reared and the wooden chair at the foot of the bed tilted and twirled. Watching that nightmare unfold in the little man's shoebox of a room awakened in me the same queasy prickle of enchantment I'd felt as a kid, looking down on a play-pretend world.

During that ninth year of my childhood, in my own bed at night, I'd hear a babbling in my head, a deep hoarse muttering that almost made sense and filled me with such terror and yearning that, if I'd been at all religious, I might have thought it was the voice of God grumbling at me. Even after my visions and voices were exposed for what they were, they still had that power to pin me shivering to my bed. Fearful as they could be, I loved them and held them in awe, believing them to be glimpses of a secret from the beyond that had chosen to reveal itself only to me, special me.

You'd think I'd have told someone about all these sinister and miraculous goings-on. And once I did. The day after I'd zipped up to the rafters, I told my baby sister, Tenley, that I could leave my body and fly. She was only four at the time but perfectly capable of raising a skeptical eyebrow and suggesting I jump off the top of our carport to prove it. I figured the leap might trick my body into taking flight before it could slam to the ground, so I took the gamble, went barreling off the gravel roof, arms spread like Superboy, and dropped like Wile E. Coyote tied to an anvil. When I hiked myself to my knees, the scorn in Tenley's eyes made me feel silly as hell. For the rest of that year, until they turned menacing, I kept the existence of my visions strictly to myself. I took to thinking of them as fragile wonders, like the locked, forgotten garden in my favorite book. If I didn't keep them private, shield them from idle prying, ridicule, or disbelief, they'd wither into dust, the same way my own secret heart would wither if I ever admitted aloud the longing for other little girls that was growing there.

Boys were my buddies and playmates. They were as matter-of-fact and sneaky about sexual experimentation as I was, and we traded peeks and fondles and rubs as intently and swiftly as we traded baseball cards. There was no room for the finer emotions in what we did, so we never suffered remorse or wounded feelings. We'd get the urge, slip off into some secluded part of a garage or basement or the great outdoors, do our business, and then hustle back to whatever game we'd interrupted. I felt the boys and I had an understanding. It was the girls who unnerved me. They seemed possessed of a keener intelligence that made me shiver, as if they weren't quite real, as if they, too, were part of the netherworld that whispered in my ear and swept me into the blue. I wanted to reach out and stroke their hair or bump their cheeks with my nose or insinuate myself into the crook of their arms, anything to make sure they were flesh and breathing and somehow mine. But I didn't dare. I was stopped cold by the same caution that made me hold my tongue every time I was hauled into the air.

In the family chronicles, I was the infant who loved to be touched and cried to be held; the baby who would turn to perfect strangers with her arms outstretched; the little girl to whom her grandmother once complained, "You are the most *affectionate* child I've ever known." That anxious impulse to connect has been lifelong, and during one bitter stretch of my young life, when I blamed that urge for all my heart's confusion, I imagined it as another side effect of the necessary drug that wreaked havoc on my fetal nervous system and, later, like some evil curse, turned the body I loved into an object of loathing. When I was in my teens, though, I came to understand that urge a little more clearly from a story my father told about his eldest sister, A-del. She was sick with diabetes, ages old, her legs gone, her teeth gone, her mind gone, but when my parents walked into her room at the nursing home, A-del seized my mother's hand and stroked it like a pet, repeating endlessly, sincerely, "I love you I love you I love you." A-del's impulse to clutch and hold and evoke love while enduring the humiliations of age and its wasting struck me then as heroic, something my own snarled heart might aspire to in its ongoing battle with the unspeakable shame of having a body. How A-del turned her humiliation into love I still don't know and fear I will never learn, because my particular humiliations of the flesh, now as when I was a child, keep threatening to churn into bitter meanness.

As a nine-year-old, disgruntled by the muddle of my body and desires, I kept my psyche's mean streak in check the way children usually do—by playing games of pretend that let me explore my more personal extremes in doses and at a remove. Intensely lovable, wickedly cunning, deeply wise—I'd play all those things to a tee if only for twenty minutes at a turn. In neighborhood games I was first choice to be Joan of Arc, because I liked being roped to a tree, and when the imaginary fires were burning me to a crisp, I'd howl so piteously, so loudly, and for so long that my inquisitors fell to their knees stunned as cows, the wrath of God smiting their secretly wicked child hearts. I was the favored fugitive from a chain gang because I picked the dankest, filthiest, most improbable hiding places, and when finally caught I put up enough fuss, as the citizen mob dragged me along the ground, to turn the hysteria of our game into something frenzied and real. At school I couldn't wait to make a commotion, and headed straight for drama club. I could be one scary little kid, damp and lisping with need until my teachers gave me the male roles the boys my age scorned, like dorky, pantaloon-wearing Wilbur in the series of plays that bore his name. No matter how they cast me, I'd find some excuse to fall flat on my butt violently enough to shake the stage, and if the stage directions read *laugh* or *cry* I'd guffaw myself into hiccups or wail until snot shot out of my nose. I played out all my frenzied alter egos while under the bright lights of the cafeteria stage or out on the green, green grass with my friends or alone in my claustrophobic bedroom or wherever else my churning mind could take me. All the world a stage, and I was hell-bent on using it as such.

Those were the years I developed my hunger for stories about the outer dark, that ether between where my body sat and my mind beheld. That's when the love grew in me for tragic family histories my parents told and retold, stories that seemed to shift their mysteries depending upon what I yearned to hear—so that the sudden death of an infant was in one telling about a mother's grief and in another about a premonition that was all but useless because it came too late. I checked out every book in the children's section of the Fort Hood army base library that seemed to echo my own fraught state of being, reading and rereading them until I could recite their longer passages like prayers. Stories about children snatched by tunneling winds right out of their ordinary lives or of prescient siblings battling forces of time so sinister and subtle that no adult could perceive them or of difficult, unpretty little girls waking up, dry-eyed and watchful, to a world that had died or left them. It was then, during my body's most urgent time of turmoil and change, that the belief arose in me to which I still cling: that somewhere in the thicket of all those words I kept struggling to hear and feared to pronounce was the key to my own story, if only I could find it.

PART I

Drowning

Them and Me

I DON'T KNOW if it was morning or evening when the doctor injected my gorgeous little mother with a mycin antibiotic. That part of the story never registered with me. I do know she was six months pregnant with me when she entered the American military field hospital in Stuttgart, Germany, although her figure was so trim, the admitting nurse refused to believe she was pregnant, much less in her second trimester. And I know from the countdown on my fingers that the fateful moment had to have occurred in July, even though I've always imagined it bracketed by weather dark and coldly foreboding. Stuttgart was where my father, Paul, had been sent to spy by the U.S. Army Counter Intelligence Corps after World War II. My mother, Edna, was in a field hospital there because she'd developed a nasty kidney infection. "Field hospital" always makes me think of some MASH with a blood-soaked, packed-dirt floor, but this one, judging from the image of it on my birth certificate, was a staid, unornamented square of brick that the American military had claimed as a spoil of war.

As Mother tells it, when the doctor came into her

room, she was reading a book (I once told this story saying she was reading a movie magazine and Mother objected, saying it made her sound like some bimbo, so I changed it back). So, she was in her bed reading a *book* and put it aside while the doctor, who looked a little like Elmer Fudd, shot her up with the antibiotic. He then checked her pulse, checked mine, marked her stomach with a big red *X* where my heart beat, and left us there. The doctor had just gone out the door, my mother says, when she felt me turn in her belly. As I did, she could feel her feet go cold and then icy as a chill started moving up and up her body. The chill had almost reached her heart before she realized she was dying. She buzzed for the nurse and then she couldn't move anymore. The nurse came in, took one look, and panicked. "Oh, Mrs. Galloway! What is it? What is it?" She could find no pulse. My mother was in a private room with huge French windows that opened onto a balcony, and after the nurse went running for the doctor, my mother thought, *If only he will open those windows, maybe I can breathe.* Right when she had that thought, the doctor walked back into her room. He didn't say one word. He just looked down into her eyes as if what she was thinking was clear as a voice in his ear, then turned on his heel and opened the windows. When he did, she felt her pulse (and mine) begin again.

A year earlier, a continent away, American medicos had already discovered that pregnant women who were given the antibiotic called mycin suffered unforeseen complications, most of them to the fetus. When I was up and grown I asked my mother, during one of our 2 a.m. confidentials, if the military hospitals in Europe, the ones caring for the American troops and their families, had used the mycin knowingly. We were sitting on the green molded-plastic lawn chairs out in the garage of her Texas ranchetta, where Mother likes to smoke. She took an illicit puff of her little cigar (she'd just had a quadruple bypass) and said, "Oh, they knew about it all right. I used to think it was just another one of those sneaky, underhanded tricks they were always pulling back then, you know, like thalidomide. But when you were older your daddy and I read a book about it. They *were* being kind of sneaky, because they knew the risks of that drug to the fetus and they didn't bother to tell us. But doctors back then didn't have all that many options for treating things like kidney infections, and mine was a bad one. If they hadn't used that mycin on me, I might have died and you right along with me. So there you go."

In all my decades of listening to my own life story, that was the first I'd heard of that. I'd grown up with the distinct impression that the doctor who poked us with the needle was a lying snake who had deliberately set out to harm us. This new information so surprised the talk out of me I forgot to ask the question I was dying to: if he *had* told her the consequences of the drug, what would she have chosen?

As it is, I remain grateful to have made it out of the womb alive, and whenever Mother tells the story about the doctor opening the window, I cry at the happy outcome. Only at those times when I am feeling gloomy do I fasten on the one detail—the baby turning in her belly. I keep thinking the fetal me must have felt that chemical torrent coming and tried hard as hell to get out of its way.

The only other untoward incident in the saga of my birth occurred October 31, the morning I was born. I was coming out in the corridor on the way to the delivery room and for some reason Mother's doctor took my early appearance as a personal affront. He didn't want me to be born in the corridor but in the delivery room, where propriety dictated I should be born. In order to keep me contained within that short stretch of linoleum longer, Dr. Fudd took my mother's legs and crossed them at the ankles. He might as well have pinched my face in a vise. When I was finally pulled out of there, my features were as accordioned as a shar-pei's and my nose was a swollen purple.

My daddy, though a handsome man (Mother says he was a perfect mix of William Holden and Frank Sinatra), had something of a purplely swollen nose himself and when he first laid eyes on me he laughed like he'd been punched in the gut. "Good God, Edna," he said. "The poor little stinker looks just like me." Mother didn't find it one bit funny. When she felt my face being pressured into her thighs, she'd spat and cursed that doctor, a fucking Major, with the foulest words she could think of (and she could think of quite a few). It still rankles her that she couldn't unhook her legs to kick him in the balls.

I've never been too happy with my nose. The worst of the swelling has gone down somewhat but there's no denying the tip's still round. As it was, I made my entrance as comic relief, and the interior tragedy of my screwed-up fetal nervous system didn't make itself known right then and there. If it had, who knows that I'd even be here to write this. From the stories I swap with my disabled friends, I know that the physical facts of an infant's body can determine the welcome that baby receives, even the ones lucky enough to be born smack in the middle of the US of A. Over margaritas, my friend Laura recently told me about the day in a Texas hospital in the early seventies that she was born with foreshortened arms, hands like flippers, and a lower body that would need a brace to straighten it out. Her mother's obstetrician didn't do the usual things my mother's did with me—wipe her off, suction her nose, spank her bottom. He just stared blankly at Laura's little baby body, then leaned over and whispered to her mother that if she wanted, he'd put the thing aside.

Stories like that do a lot to fuel my paranoid sense that every corner of the world has a mean streak even a baby has got to be prepared to survive. Which may be why I find parallels most people don't between the stories my disabled friends tell about their narrow escapes and the stories my mother tells about living with Daddy and my older sister, Trudy, in post-Nazi Germany when she was pregnant with me. "You got to understand," Mother told us three girls when we were grown and gathered in the kitchen of her Texas ranchetta late one night, "what it was like arriving in that place, knowing what we did about what those German skunks had done to the Jews. When we first came to Stuttgart it was just a handful of years after the war and that place was all bombed out. Rubble everywhere you looked. But the factories were still running, belching out smoke day and night. The three of us, Daddy, me, and Trudy, we moved around until they finally put us up in a requisitioned two-story house. Yeah, we'd taken it from the Germans, but the Germans had stolen it first from the Jews. The furnace of that house was in the kitchen. It was meant to heat both floors, so it was huge. Your daddy was gone doing his spy stuff most of the time, and by then I was nearing my last month and about as big as the dining room table. I couldn't handle that furnace all by myself, so Military Command assigned us a German, an ex-Nazi infantryman, to run it. What he was, was a stoker. But we called him the Fireman. The Fireman had his own key to the place. He'd come in the morning right after Daddy had taken Trudy to elementary school, while I was still asleep, and the click of the latch would wake me up. I knew he was trying to be quiet, tap tap tapping in his boots across the tile. I knew he was trying not to disturb me, but it gave me the creeps. I'd get up and go downstairs just to be sure, just to see for myself, and there he'd be, kneeling down by the furnace, his face all red from the heat. Seeing him crouched there, feeding the fires like that, knowing what his people had done, that would have been enough. But then he'd look up at me—those pale little eyes of his never quite catching mine—and he'd grin. Nod his head and grin. I could never tell if that grin was polite or mocking. It was like he was saying, 'You win. But be careful sleeping.'

"And it wasn't just that one thing," Mother said, trying to make us, her now grown daughters, understand the urgency of the distrust that had mystified us as children. "It was everything. You could smell their defeat. I mean that literally. You'd walk down the street and they all looked unbathed, their hair unwashed, their clothes all filthy, like they'd given up, didn't care how bad they stunk. I had to pour on the perfume before I could walk out the door. And they knew me for what I was. American. Dressed too good, looked too clean, looked like I ate. We'd beaten them, so we had the food, the clothes, all the money and the hope, and they hated us for it.

"This one day, when I was in that last month with Terry and, like I said, really, really big, I took a bus to food shop or something, I don't remember what. The minute I got on I could feel the hate. The bus was crowded and hot and stunk, and they were all looking at me like I was some kind of bug. And then they started pushing. It wasn't even a conscious thing, I think. I was standing there right at the lip of the steps, that bus speeding along, and they just did it, all of them, started nudging me, crowding me, pushing me back, trying to push me, a pregnant woman, right out that open door. The driver, he was watching it all happen in his mirror and he wasn't going to stop or even slow down. He was in on it, too."

Trudy, who like me had loved her childhood years in Germany, took a quick bite of brownie and fixed Mother with her scholar's gaze. "But you made it," she said with a hint of defensiveness. "You survived." To which Mother replied with a sharp *huh* of anger, "Yeah. We made it. No thanks to *them*."

"Lucky to have made it no thanks to them" is a popular mantra among my disabled friends, the *them* shifting with the circumstance, the story. They can be upper-class parents who stick you in an institution when you're a toddler because your spine twists where it shouldn't; or scientists who conduct thirty-six exploratory operations so they can test their theories on your eleven-year-old body; or just superstitious passersby who gawk at the newborn you like you're some kind of nasty insect and they wish they had a swatter. Their insufferable self-regard and trumped-up cultural standards of purity are a shallow disguise. Look deeply enough into their eyes and you'll see the smoldering loathing of their own flesh that flares fast into meanness toward you. Beware *them*. Steel yourself against *them*. They are everywhere and won't hesitate to put the imperfect infant aside or crowd a pregnant woman off the lip of a speeding bus. They can even be you, hating your own screwed-up body, wanting it dead.

As a still seemingly normal child growing up in Germany, I had already cultivated a well-developed, suspicious distrust of *them,* whoever they might prove to be, long before it had been figured out that I was deaf, long before the hallucinations kicked in. For that I have to thank, in part, our German maid, Edith. After we were restationed to Berlin in 1954, Edith was hired through the Marshall Plan to clean and cook for our family, to watch my new baby sister, Tenley, and to keep me, the middle daughter, company. From the stories she told, I thought *they* were the Russians, the Commies that my daddy spied on and Edith feared. Edith was a skinny, bespectacled, stoop-shouldered woman with a frizz of mud-brown hair. She was a constant reader and would later study literature at the Free University of Berlin. I used to press my nose against the thick, seldom-washed woolen sweater she wore and breathe her in deep. I loved the aromas ingrained there of fried onions, peeled oranges, and her own delicious sweat. I called her "my Edith." My Edith's family and her fiancé, a German army infantryman, had all been wiped out during the war. There was nothing left of them but her memories, and at night, when I had trouble falling asleep, she'd stroke my back and share them with me.

"I am playing in the yard with my brother when my father, he come say, 'Go hide. The Russians,' he say. 'The Russians!' We all go to the cellar and above we hear them. They are smashing things in our house. When they have enough smashing they shoot, at the ceiling, the wall, at nothing, they are shooting into the floor. A bullet comes down *bang!* into the cellar, there by my foot. They are hoping to kill us but they are too much lazy to look. Stupid, those Russians, hmm? Still wanting to kill us. Now sleep, my *liebchen,* sleep."

When we girls were grown and my mother retold my Edith's stories, she'd use a chopped-up comic variant of English, like Colonel Klink in *Hogan's Heroes*: "I am playing in der yard mit my brudder." But that was because she thought Edith was crazy as a loon, "telling a child bedtime stories like that." Mother never believes me when I tell her I had loved the anxieties those stories awoke in me. They offset the more immediate one, the real-life *them* that lay in wait just a few miles to the east of us.

Edith's stories had the same effect on me as our favorite family game, Scare. My sister Trudy, the ponytailed, spectacle-wearing, beloved boss-of-us-all at school, play yard, and home, is the one who gave Scare its name. But Daddy was the one who set its tone. Scare with the Galloways was not your usual game of hide-and-seek but something far more intense, even a little sinister.

We three girls were always the prey during this late-night game, and the role of our parents was to find us out. They'd take turns stalking us after we'd hidden, one of them reading in the living room with the door shut while the other prowled the back of the darkened apartment. Our family played the game so often we girls became sophisticated in our hiding places—no behind-the-doors or under-the-beds for us. We'd sandwich ourselves between the slats and the springs instead, or climb up the shelves of the linen closet and burrow behind the heaps of folded towels, or curl our bodies so tight they'd fit into the packing trunks, the mothballed sweaters layered over us innocent and undisturbed. Then we'd wait.

Mother was like a princess out of *Grimms' Fairy Tales*—hair black as night, eyes green as emeralds, skin white as snow—but when she was *them* she looked more wicked than any witch in the book. She had beautiful full lips that always seemed painted a lavish red and her teeth had been made perfect by German dentistry. She'd fix her smile into the bright-toothed, lapping grin of a clever, hungry wolf and call out to us, her little chickens, to come to their mommy, who loved them, turning the word "love" into a growling croon that made us shiver.

When Daddy was *them* the whole apartment turned still. He hunted like a spider, hunched over, his weight on the tips of his fingers and toes, skittering quietly through the dark. Daddy liked to toy with his prey, let us hang there, wondering. Letting us suspect. Letting the question of his hidden presence tantalize us until every creak, every shift of light, every prickling of our skin became *them*. We didn't know then that we were playing with a master, that Daddy was a covert operative who, when he disappeared from home for days at a time, played his own brand of Scare with the enemy in East Berlin.

We could never be sure who Daddy would be when he came home evenings from work. He'd leave us in the morning, his hair slicked back, the crisp heroism of his uniform just a little offset by the army-issue glasses perched on his nose. When he'd return that night his slicked-back hair would be parted on the right, not the left, side, and he'd be wearing a three-piece suit, his glasses tucked away in an inside pocket. Mother and Trudy knew what little Tenley and I didn't find out until we were grown. That Daddy was another man by day, a German named Herr Gault, who worked in East, not West, Berlin. There he moved among the Soviets, just another anonymous, whistling *Beamt* going about his business, even as he was singling out the traitors, the turncoats, the double agents, and having them silenced or even—although to this day whenever we girls suggest it, Mother screws her eyes tight and shakes her head no, no, no—doing the deed himself. We might not have known the particulars of Daddy's job then, but Scare felt different when we played with him. When he stalked us we seldom giggled or sneezed or shifted or sighed but played as if something really were at stake. Like our lives.

My family has continued to play this game of Scare throughout the years, although we put it aside the August my father died at age eighty-seven. The neuroglioblastoma covering his brain like a hand had him believing he'd been kidnapped by East Berlin operatives. His first night in the hospital he kept looking for makeshift weapons and telling my mother and Tenley, who had followed the ambulance, to get out while they could. Later, as he lay dying back at the Texas ranch he'd built himself by hand, he muttered things mother didn't want to hear. "Of the eleven," he said once, "only I escaped." And he kept whispering, among other things, "It all had to be done."

Scare as we played it back during the Cold War strikes me now as having been some kind of weird, half-conscious preparation, a dress rehearsal, maybe, for the Communist invasion everyone in West Berlin was sure would come. I always thought the tricks we learned from playing with Daddy—how to choose the unexpected hiding place, how to calm our ragged breathing once we'd hidden, how to

hold our bodies so still that we could almost negate ourselves—could very well have saved us if the Soviets attacked, like the silly song my Edith taught us children to
sing in Russian. "If they catch you," she said, as we warbled
foreign words to the tune of "The Old Gray Mare," "und
you sing this song then maybe they don't shoot you dead."

At the German-American school Trudy and I attended,
our principal, Mr. Faye, called a morning assembly to give
us instructions in case of the Unlikely Event. We would
know the Communists were invading, he said, by the deep,
constant *ou-wah ou-wah* (a sound he imitated) of a siren.
Judging from the sweat beading his lip he seemed certain
the *ou-wahing* would start within the hour. If we happened
to be at the school when we heard those sirens we'd simply follow our teacher's good example and hide under
our desks. If Armageddon sounded outside of school, we
were to run straight home to our mothers. Our mothers,
it seemed, had been ordered by American Military Command to keep a special suitcase packed and stored under
their beds for just such a doomsday emergency. Suitcases in
hand, our mothers would then take us to the parking lot of
the Am Hegewinkel apartments, where all the American
dependents lived. A fleet of big, olive-green army transport trucks would be idling there, ready to whisk us to the
Templehof airport, where we would make our final escape
by plane. Our fathers, the principal assured us, the sweat
dripping from him now, would meet us in a place of safety
as time permitted.

Our father, privy to every secret, knew time wouldn't
permit. He knew we were so close to enemy territory, the
Russian snipers could pick us off as we were running for
the trucks. If by some miracle we did manage to elude the

first wave of invaders, the road to the Tempelhof airport, our one route of escape, ran parallel to the Soviet artillery range in Potsdam. Missiles belonging to *them* had long been armed and aimed at that road and anything traveling on it.

We girls knew none of Daddy's secrets then, but I had already discovered one of my own during a game of Scare. I'd pulled the blue vinyl suitcase out from under my parents' bed, intending to dump the essentials and curl myself inside. It was empty. I scooted it over to the plastic clothes hamper, hoping it would seem less out of place to the searching eye, crawled in, pulled it shut, then lay there in a ball, pondering. Child or no, I realized what that empty blue suitcase was telling me. The same thing as the principal's sweat. Which was probably why I could never imagine running home to Mother or boarding those trucks or flying away from harm; why the only image I could conjure of that day of reckoning was of my father, sirens *ou-wahing* all around, sitting at his office desk, hands folded, head bowed. If the suitcase under my mother's bed was empty, I knew good and well there could be no plan, no logic, no real place of safety or escape.

I like to think my handful of years living in that jittery city on the verge, with all its threats of *them*—both real and play-pretend—toughened me up, readied me to survive what would soon become a shifting, hallucinatory, and deafening childhood. There are games within games being played out in life, and if you aren't careful or you're no good at playing them or you just run out of luck, too bad for you—I believed that even then, blossoming hard case that I was. I can see that mean streak unfolding in the story my family loves to tell about a twelve-year-old friend of Trudy's in Berlin who came to spend the night and, at our urging, asked Daddy to play Scare with us. She wouldn't play, though, unless she got to choose our hiding place and we three sisters hid there with her. Her choice proved dangerously unimaginative. Under our parents' bed. There was no dissuading the fool. But as we huddled under there together, pressed between the bed slats and the naked floor, waiting in the dark silence for the Monster to stalk and (inevitably, his daughters knew) to find us, she must have sensed the lethal imprudence of her own stupid choice, because suddenly, overcome by nothing, nothing at all, she fell into a crying fit and wet her pants.

I'd just turned seven but at the smell of her I could almost feel the blank drop of my own face, an expression (new to me then) of contempt. But I was being not at all cruel to that yelping, peeing friend of ours—who was, after all, older than I; whose parents, after all, would have to be roused from their beds to come hustle that big baby home to the excessive and bogus safety of their lives—when I whispered, in a voice so flat as to be almost venomous, "If this hadn't been a game, you'd be dead."

Visions

WHEN MY GRANNY DORIS WAS A YOUNG, sweet-faced, blue-eyed little mother, she lived with her husband and four children in a way-out-in-the-middle-of-nowhere place in Texas called Rattlesnake Canyon. It wasn't called Rattlesnake Canyon for nothing. Rattlers, copperheads, cottonmouths lurked everywhere you looked. Her husband, Charles, a short, tough, hazel-eyed Irishman, burnt a circle in the grass around the house so Doris could hang her wash and the older three kids could play without some slithering son of a bitch sneaking up on them.

One cold dawn two days after Christmas, Doris got up, as usual, to feed her husband breakfast and send him off to his job. Charles was a roughneck for the Boaz Oil Company, working the Number Ten, a rig that was maybe sixty miles from the company-owned home where he and Doris lived. She gave him his kiss and stood in the yard waving him goodbye until the battered black truck he drove was just a speck in her sight. She left her muddied slippers on the porch; so she was barefoot when she went in to check on the baby, Robert, who'd had a touch of colic.

When I was first told this story, I imagined everything after Doris went back into the house happening in slow-motion and reverential silence. But my mother, Edna, who was then going on twelve and shared a room with the baby, now tells me, "No. It was the screaming that woke me up." She reared up in bed, still half-asleep, to see her own mother, Doris, standing in the doorway of the bedroom—barefoot, beautiful in her nightgown, her hair still unloosed to her waist—screaming her head off. By the gray light of the window my mother could see the baby, Robert, unmoving in his crib, a small, blue, last breath bubble still hanging from his little nose. Then her mother snatched that baby up, ran out of the room, out of the house, and kept on running, barefoot, just as dawn was breaking, through Rattlesnake Canyon.

"In the commotion of all that followed," my mother told me, "it was like I was in a different world." She can't remember how long she and her two other brothers were alone in that house, who found them there, or how their father got word. What she does know is that when her father finally found her mother huddled in a deep crevasse of the canyon it was almost dark and Doris wouldn't let her husband pry the baby out of her arms. My mother was old enough to know what happens to the body when it dies. And she could hardly bear to think of her mother out there for all those hours, holding that tiny one, feeling the changes.

The year I turned nine, that became my favorite family story. I'd pester my mother to tell it late at night when we girls didn't have any particular reason to be up the next morning. My interest bordered on obsessive, but it's easy to understand why it resonated so deeply with me then.

That was the year I began feeling the changes to my own body that seemed as mysterious and inevitable to me as dying, even though they were nothing I could pinpoint or explain.

In 1958 we left Berlin, traveling by train in the dead of winter in the dead of night over the Soviet border into Frankfurt, where we caught the plane that flew us to New Jersey. From there we drove west the thousand miles to Fort Hood, Texas, where Daddy had been stationed. My mother's people came from the east-central Texas cattle and oil lands, so during the whole trip there I was falling in love with my notion of the state, which I had glimpsed only once before on a visit to our grandparents when I was five. The Fort Hood of my daydreams was a Fort Apache, with snorting horses, whipping flags, and stagecoaches on the run from the Chiricahuas.

Fort Hood, the reality, was a scrubby, brown-baked, sprawling outpost in the middle of nowhere, nary a horse in sight. Our first unromantic year there, we lived in temporary housing in neighboring Killeen. By spring of the next we'd moved into a spanking new, prefabricated military family house on the army base. It was there I began the odd practice of lifting out of my body. The first time my body and I parted ways, it seemed so much like a recurring dream of mine, I thought I had to be asleep. In that dream, *they* were invading the apartment complex where we lived in Berlin, and Daddy and my Edith were leading us to safety, down a hidden staircase that had miraculously displaced the small, cold back bathroom of our apartment, where Mother kept the cat litter pan. We were halfway down the stairs when Mother realized I'd forgotten the baby—she had given me little Tenley to hold. I ran back up to our apartment and was just reaching down to pick the baby off the floor where I'd left her when the door splintered open and *they* poured in, dressed in dark utilitarian uniforms, eager to kill us. In that dream, as later, awake, my mind fled to the ceiling and clung there, an invisible, untouchable witness to it all. My body and the baby? Both safe, I hoped.

But this new thing that was now happening to me was no dream. When I'd drop down back into myself, my body was always right in the middle of whatever it had been doing the minute before—running a race or teasing one of my prissy girl classmates or idly tracking the Milky Way. In the beginning, I pretended these odd displacements were Merlin-like charms allowing me a glimpse into the divine. I was driven to keep them secret, because the one time I had tried telling my baby sister I could fly, the eloquence, the beauty of those spells became a kind of slapstick—me falling off the roof of the carport and little Tenley witnessing my failure with a flat, sneering look in her eyes. I didn't want my enchantments sullied or mocked. They were mine. They were beautiful. And they would someday reveal something so miraculous to me that other people, if only they knew, would beg to fly out of their bodies, too.

Then one spring night, more than half a year after they'd begun, the nature of my enchantment changed. Fort Hood was celebrating some occasion, probably Memorial Day, with fireworks. Our family and neighbors were gathered in our front yard, blankets spread out on the lawn, lawn chairs unfolded on the carport. I liked sitting on the trunk of our black 1960 Ford and that's where I was when it happened. I was admiring the spinning blast of a whirling dragon when I was lifted away from my body into that place I had come from habit to recognize—a gray, substanceless space through which I could see, as through a tunnel, my own body, sitting just as I'd left it. But this time, for the first time, I wasn't alone in there. There was a shadow, a small, child-shaped thicket of darkness, in there with me.

Tenley has a story she tells now from her days working for animal control, about the time the code enforcers brought a wolf hybrid to the kennels. All the other breeds went wild at the smell, barking, yapping, snapping at the air, until the wolf-dog, bored with the commotion, hiked himself up on his haunches and let loose a howl. The silence that followed was immediate. When Tenley looked around she saw that every dog in the kennel had flattened to its belly. I felt exactly like those cowering dogs when I first glimpsed that shadow. It was no bigger than I but radiated an energy so primitive and malevolent it might as well have howled. When it whipped around as if it sensed me, my instinct was to flatten. I needn't have bothered. It had fixed its savage attention beyond me, on the second image I was making—my body sitting empty and vulnerable on the trunk of the car. It meant to inhabit my vacant body, and if it did I knew I would no longer be myself, the person I thought of as *I* would be left behind in that vague twilight. What followed was a feeling so instant and complete it became a kind of action, a headlong rush. And I was on the trunk of our car again, above me the same great sparkling burst. I looked down at my fingers, then jumped off the car, ran straight to my mother, and finally told her, "I can fly. I can leave my body and fly."

My mother had been born in a small town in Texas called Thrift, and my father in an even smaller Alabama town called Eclectic. They'd met in New Mexico, married, and traveled a military route, riding the trains from one army camp to another throughout World War II. They'd lived all over the United States and in parts of Europe. They enjoyed a party. My mother would often sing in the officers' clubs. My father loved languages and chess. All those years on the road, they had been trading their rural childhoods for something new. Even so, when I came running to them that night, it wasn't diagnosis that first came to their minds when I swore I had been snatched out of my body—it was the old stories of the uncanny. There were plenty of them on both sides of the family. The other half of the Rattlesnake Canyon story, for instance, which my mother tells as an epilogue but always struck me as a preface.

The Christmas of 1935 my Great-Grandmother Eve and her sister Eve (twins who spelled their names the same but pronounced them differently) had come down from Burkburnett, Texas, to spend the holiday with Great-Grandma Eve's son Charles, or Chuck, as he was called, and his family. That was the first and last time those two were to lay eyes on the new baby, Robert. Eve, my great-aunt, called him her little birdie and nicknamed him Robin. Eve, my great-grandmother, couldn't stop marveling over how delicate he was, his skin whiter than the cotton batting under the Christmas tree. The unnatural pearliness of his skin should have told them right then what would happen, my mother says, and probably did.

The twins had been known as sensitives since the day they'd both been born with cauls, gauzy membranes that had covered their faces like veils. They were good-natured, well-bred women who hadn't hesitated to divorce their scoundrel first husbands at a time when divorce was almost as much of a sin as murder. With all those marriages between them, they never felt their reputation for extrasensory wisdom was really deserved. Although, my mother claims the most insightful bit of advice she ever got about prospective mates came from my Great-Aunt Eve, who told her, "Imagine the boy naked, Edna. If you like the picture, he's the one for you." But all through their long lives—they lived to be ninety-three and died within three months of each other, my mother's grandma first, her aunty following from sheer loneliness—the two Eves pooh-poohed the notion that they might be seers. It was only after baby Robert died that they began wondering if maybe they did have power to foretell, even though it was really just my Great-Grandma Eve who glimpsed—that once—the shadow of a future.

The day after Christmas, the twins had taken a train back up to Burkburnett traveling northward through the night. When they'd gotten home in the wee hours of the next morning, they'd put their bags down in the hall and brewed themselves a pot of tea. My great-grandmother happened to glance down at the loose leaves in her drained cup and what she saw there made her put her precious Winterling china carefully aside: the image of a child's coffin. "Sister," she called out to Aunty, who was heading up the stairs, a suitcase in each hand, "I wouldn't bother to unpack those bags. One of the children just died."

My parents filled my life with stories like that—hushed and thrilling stories they had been told long ago, and new stories of their own. A window opening and my mother's dying heart starting up again; my father one night dreaming that Roosevelt was dead, then waking up the next morning to the news that the president had, indeed, died. Whatever the uncanny might be called—prescience or foretelling—my parents thought of it as a deep, almost molecular knowing that comes from noticing the subtle clues of something that is in fact unfolding and will soon enough make itself known. It is no wonder, then, that the night I told my parents I had left my body and flown, they simply listened to what I had to say, checked me for fever, then put me to bed. They were going to believe me. They just weren't sure how.

Presto Change-o

TWO DAYS AFTER I'D TOLD MY PARENTS I could fly, my fourth-grade elementary school teacher took my mother aside at the Tuesday-night PTA meeting. She had rearranged the seating for the class, and ever since she put me in the back row I'd been behaving oddly. I'd been an A student, always quick to answer every question, but now I just sat there looking puzzled. If I had my head down when my teacher spoke to me, I wouldn't respond at all. More than once, she reminded my mother, I'd left school during recess and showed up at home for lunch. She wondered if I might be going deaf. "My Terry?" That's all my mother could think to say, and it was more an exclamation than a question. Until I mentioned the business of flying I'd never said one word about my body feeling different or changed. She thought I was still her little chicken who loved nothing better than to sit with her in the living room while she was ironing and watch cartoons while I finished my homework. What she didn't know, because I didn't think to tell her, was that if I closed my eyes or turned my back, the voices on TV, like the voices all around me, blurred into a confusion of senseless noises, not much different from the hum of an air conditioner or the gurgle of a faulty drain.

My family thought of me as independent to the extreme, with a private streak as wide as my conflicting need to be told I was loved, which according to my mother was considerable. From the time I could walk and talk, there'd be days when I'd get under her feet while she was making dinner and pull on her shirt every handful of minutes or so and say, "I love you, Mommy," then wait like an anxious dog until she'd reply, "I love you too." My mother sometimes now berates herself for not seeing that little quirk of mine as a clue to my vanishing sense, but I've reassured her that with people in the family like poor old Aunt A-del and her endlessly repetitive I love you's, there wasn't any way she could have possibly suspected.

Body talk was distasteful to me at that age. When my mother and sister Trudy tried to sit me down for a conversation about menstruation, pregnancy, and sex, I'd turned on them, tight faced, saying, "I don't care to know about all that right now, thank you." I was afraid those two had got whiff of the fooling around I'd been doing with the neighborhood boys. I didn't want to encourage any line of thought that might lead them to the hoary evidence of my guilt surely lingering on my skin like oil. But that embarrassment with my body's clandestine sexual awakening wasn't the only reason I was being so closemouthed.

At the beginning, I'd found all my body-leaving to be as thrilling as *The Invasion of the Body Snatchers*. I liked pretending Fort Hood was rapidly filling up with pod people and that I'd soon be the last true human on the face of the earth. It gave me a somewhat paranoid sense of superiority, which I enjoyed. But then the changes kept coming.

People around me suddenly developed double profiles, and if I turned away while they were speaking they'd start jabbering in a foreign tongue. That's when I knew the alien thing—draining away words and sounds and pulling me out of the sweet, solid world I loved into some cold, remote place above it all—wasn't outside, but lurking within me. It was my body turning into a *them,* my body that was beginning to scare me.

For months I'd kept mum about my inner turmoil, hoping the commotion would disappear on its own and I'd turn back into the same little girl I'd started out as. I was sure I was on my way to being my old self again the night after I told my parents I could fly. I trusted those two to get the mess of reality sorted out and my peculiar troubles resolved, and privately, without a lot of fuss. Then, not even a week into my confession, the jig was up and I'd been outed to my whole wide world, the entire Fort Hood Elementary School fourth grade.

It was a Monday. The projector and the audiometer were already set up when we trooped back into homeroom from cafeteria lunch. Our teacher, a squinty, long-faced brunette who looked like a mule eating an apple when she talked, explained the etiquette of the two tests we were about to take. See the big *E*, make the shape of the big *E* with your fingers; hear the beep, wave your right hand. I could barely make out the first big *E* shining against the chalkboard, but that seemed a minor detail. I'd just follow the cues of the kids around me. My fingers were agile as a monkey's as they formed the various *E*'s, *W*'s and *M*'s. I was just starting to relax into lazy satisfaction—the pod people with their high-tech tricks weren't going to trip *me* up—when the test administrator, a tubby-looking man with thin, flaky hair, turned off the projector, turned on the audiometer, and issued his fateful instructions: "Put your heads down on your desks and close your eyes." My back straightened. My stomach turned. In my mind's eye I saw my immediate future—I'd be sitting at my desk dumb as a rock amid a waving field of kids. Right then and there, I knew the real weirdness of my life had only just begun.

The day after those hearing and eye tests my parents called the Fort Hood base hospital. Two days later I was undergoing a battery of tests as the doctors poked, prodded, and worked me over, following one hunch then another as they tried to pinpoint the problem. The radiologists took sheaves of X-rays. The army nurses took so much blood, I worked up a positive fondness for the needle. Kids who were howling and carrying on about their polio boosters were hauled in to witness my pincushion serenity. After those tests were finished, that batch of military medical professionals sent me and my mother on to another group of military physicians at the Fort Sam Houston hospital who did a second round of tests, including a necessary—so they told my mother—if unpleasant procedure.

Just getting to Houston had been unpleasant enough. We were a one-car family and Daddy needed the Ford for work. He dropped me and my mother off at the Fort Hood hospital parking lot to catch the 6 a.m. army bus to Fort Sam Houston. At 10:45 we arrived at the Houston branch hospital along with the eight other transport patients. For four-and-a-half hours my mother and I sat in a long corridor painted a depressing un-sunshiny yellow, on a straight-backed wooden bench with a long crack in its seat. Finally an army nurse escorted us into a room that was empty but for a leather chair, which had straps on the armrests that looked like, but couldn't possibly be, restraints. Sweat stains had turned the leather a rich chocolaty brown. To the side of the chair was a delicate-looking metal surgical stand on which sat an aluminum bowl covered with a towel. At the sight of these objects my mother and I exchanged a nervous glance and a chuckle. The nurse, who didn't seem amused, took me by the forearm and peeled me away from my mother, saying to her, "You can leave now." But Mother wasn't going anywhere. The nurse said, "You won't want to see this," then lifted me onto the chair and started buckling me in tight. When my arms had been rendered immobile she went to the door, opened it to call for the doctor, then said again to my mother, "You really won't want to see this." But she didn't insist.

I have no memory of what the doctor looked like, but when I think of him now, I see that chinless little chicken farmer of a Nazi, Heinrich Himmler. He didn't say a word to either me or my mother, not even a grunt of greeting. He just nodded to the nurse and waited impassively as she took my head by the jaw and temple, turned it to the side, and held it against the headrest. When my head was good and secure, the doctor took the towel off the bowl. I couldn't see it then, but it held a syringe and a small bucket of ice water. He filled the syringe with the ice water and injected it deep into my ear. Then the nurse released her hold. When ice water hit the tiny nerve hairs of my inner ear, the world began to spin, but really what was spinning were my eyes. I couldn't help but cry out because my perceptions had turned into a frightening, kaleidoscopic, whirling mush. I vomited. Repeatedly. It lasted a good long time. And they did it twice. The nurse told my mother yet again that she could leave the room, but Mother wouldn't budge, even though, she told my daddy and sisters late that night after we'd returned, she could hardly bring herself to breathe, seeing my eyes whirling around in my head like that.

Ice water must be a doozy of a diagnostic tool. Less than a week after that procedure, the medicine men arrived at their conclusions: "A chemical imbalance caused by the introduction of drugs to the fetal nervous system" was making me deaf. My increasing deafness combined with my myopia (which was just "severe myopia") was in all probability causing the roller-coastering state of my mind. Despite their best intentions and the latest of diagnostic procedures, they admitted they'd found nothing more than they'd known in the first place: I was going deaf. The extent of it? Profound. The prognosis? It was going to get worse. As for the hallucinations, it was hoped that once I could see and hear the way I should, they'd stop on their own accord.

The ear, nose, and throat specialist did have a theory to pursue. He thought a little flap of flesh in my throat might be a partial obstruction to my hearing or maybe even a secondary source of the deafness. He asked my parents for permission to perform a tonsillectomy. They signed the papers and in a week's time I was under ether. Even before I'd shaken off its postsurgical fumes I knew the procedure had been a flop. I had come to consciousness in the ICU ward, calling out for my mother. My throat was bleeding and raw and no matter how hard I strained I couldn't even manage a croak, but that didn't stop me from trying. Then a night nurse came to the foot of my bed, looked me straight in the eye, and waggled her finger at me while mouthing hushed, almost soundless words. She'd been just as unintelligible when she'd given me my pre-op Jell-O.

The medical establishment had no cures for what ailed me, but alas, they had remedies. What they offered were thick, translucent-framed army-issue glasses for my weak eyes, and a box-sized hearing aid with two pink wires snaking up to two flesh-colored molds plugged into my dying ears. I was already feeling out of sorts with my body, and the hallucinations had been the least of it. I'd put on some weight and become chubby as a hamster, had a Moe-like bowl haircut, and my two front teeth were fangs because I'd whacked myself in the mouth with the vacuum cleaner handle I'd used as a bazooka during a game of war. None of those changes had messed with my tomboy, inner picture of myself as a fearless little male-in-the-making. I could still slick my hair back like James Dean or suck menacingly on my teeth like Dracula or make the fat of my arm pop like a muscle. These other two things were something else again. The glasses were cat shaped, with lenses as thick as a cow's tongue. The hearing aid fit into a halter that wrapped around my trainer bra, which I had only recently, and none too willingly, been convinced I ought to wear. I'd been royally pissed off about the presence of the two nubs on my chest from the minute they first popped out. And now I seemed to have acquired an unwelcome third, only this extra was square and beeped like a reversing truck every step I took. It was impossible to imagine myself a soldier, cowboy, or spy when I couldn't wriggle on my stomach through enemy lines, or gallop, whooping on my pony, to take the bad guys by surprise, or sneak past the open door where evil lay in wait. When I thought of myself in the third person the only image I could conjure was of a toad—a tubby, moist, myopic croaker who couldn't take a hop without her glasses fogging up, her boobs flopping like tiny rice-filled socks, and her hearing aid squealing like the brakes of a train. It was a sorry transformation and seemed to happen overnight. Actually, it happened in less than an hour.

My mother was the one who usually took me to be examined, but she'd begged off this last visit, telling Daddy she couldn't face another all-day marathon. I think she suspected what was coming. This grand day it was my father who drove me to Fort Sam Houston in our own car. I found it such a treat to be zipping down the highway, just him and me alone. As we went into the hospital together I was skipping up the steps, humming with happy possessiveness. My daddy, mine. An hour later I came walking back like an arthritic old lady, tentatively, suspiciously, hanging on to the rail, tapping the edge of the steps with my shoe. I had been rehearsing that little show in my mind the forty minutes it had taken them to adjust the glasses and hearing aids. I wanted my daddy to see how weighted down I felt by all the paraphernalia so he'd feel obliged to save me from it all, although I knew good and well that wasn't really something he could do.

But there was more than just panicked spitefulness running through my head as I hobbled down those steps. The remedies that were meant to set me straight felt like a patchwork of scarlet As making the private failings of my body visible for all to see; and I was sure the whole world was looking. Under the immensity of that gaze every grandiose notion I'd secretly harbored about myself—that maybe I was something of a seer, maybe I was destined to reveal some amazing hitherto unknowns, maybe a voice from the beyond really was speaking through me—was recast in my mind so swiftly I could feel the shame flare up and burn right through my body. In my new doofus guise the only destiny I had a right to expect was to be the butt of a joke.

I had suspected as much when the doctor began adjusting the quarter-inch-thick lenses, buckling the white linen pocket-halter to my torso, connecting the pink wires of the box to the plastic molds plugged into my ears. And I'd been steeling myself for the shock of exposure I knew was coming. But my daddy wasn't prepared for the sight. As he watched me make my halting way down the steps, he sat down on the top one, took his own glasses off, and began to cry. I remember looking up at him sitting there bawling his eyes out. I didn't help matters by asking him in a high, hurt voice, "Will I be like this forever?" It was a cruel thing to do, but I remember feeling cool about his tears. The reptilian heart of me was taking a far colder look at the circumstances than my daddy was. Remembering myself as I was then, I can well imagine my reasoning. Something along the lines of, *This next part of my life is gonna suck. I bet I can milk it for every tear it's worth.* I was right on both counts.

Meaner

I NEVER FELT ENVY until I was almost ten and saw Patty Duke as deaf-blind Helen Keller in *The Miracle Worker*. That girl was a sight. Her hair a greasy, matted nest, filth smeared all over her scabby little body, her cotton jumper like the rag of an urchin. Patty as Helen was as ill-willed and determined and narcissistic as I'd always dreamed of being, and bored into a spitting-mad whirlwind. She was one nasty cookie, and I knew I had it in me to be just like her. Playing Patty Duke as Helen Keller became my private game. Taking off my hearing aids and glasses and letting the inner me rip.

I loved patting my way around my room, my eyes screwed to flickering slits, my tongue tucked to the back of my throat so that every utterance I made sounded half-choked and slobbering. But the great outdoors held more potential for drama. I'd fall on the muddier parts of the backyard, which was pretty much denuded by our too-energetic-by-far black-and-white terrier, Britt, and thrash around until my clothes were good and caked. Then I'd grab handfuls of the patchy St. Augustine grass growing in the corners of the fence and rub them against my face in a desperate effort to "make sense" of where I was. I'd pat and stumble my deaf-blind way to the spigot and diddle with it until it started to drip, then pour, then spew. All the while I'd be muttering gabble until finally it would hit me, and light would dawn over my puzzled monkey face. "Wah-wah?" I'd ask. I'd pretend that, just like in the movie, it was the crucial question. I'd ask it again and louder: "Wah-wah?!" Since neither Tenley nor any of my friends were remotely interested in playing Helen's mentor and tormenter, Annie Sullivan, I was always alone in this game. But even though I couldn't see or hear Annie, I'd act as if she were out there listening anyway, just as intent on answering that question as I was. In my mind, Annie didn't look like her Anne Bancroft film version but like all the older girls I'd ever had a crush on. And if I finally got the connection between the word "wah-wah" and the stuff running over and between my fingers, the prize would be mine—their sympathetic attention to my terrible handicap and their awed admiration for my wounded but undaunted soul. An answer to my bubbling desire, and a way to be both hero and saved.

Whenever it was time for dinner and I'd have to get civilized again, it always felt wrong to be clean, combed, and calmed down. Since being diagnosed and "fixed," I'd felt miffed as a neutered tom. I was mad as hell that I had to wear the glasses and hearing aids, not just because they made me look ugly but because they slowed me down. I couldn't run or even trot without the glasses misting up or the hearing aids bouncing and beeping. Spur-of-the-minute physical fun and feral daring were nixed. I couldn't detour through some neighbor's sprinkler or butt one of my friends in the belly or run around shrieking in the rain. I had to think first, which I hated to do, because the hearing aids were fragile and expensive and wouldn't survive a spontaneous jump in a puddle. One wrong move on my part meant hundreds of bucks down the drain, and that knowledge, besides cramping my style, was making me surly and self-pitying.

My mother was a petite, raven-haired beauty. My daddy, a handsome, soft-eyed if shorter than average soldier, resplendent in his uniform. My big sister, Trudy, with her almond-shaped eyes of gray, her waist-length chestnut ponytail, and her wrestler's calves, had been elected head cheerleader of the Killeen High School Kangaroos, and she'd even been crowned *Miss* Kangaroo. My cute-as-a-button, doe-eyed, dark-haired flirt of a baby sister, Tenley, had just that summer been crowned a Little Miss Aqua Fest. Then there was me. I knew by all rights I ought to have been up there in the pantheon of family charmers instead of stuck in my new identity as child freak. I'd stand in front of the mirror, assessing my chances for a happy life. They seemed on par with one of those *hyuck-hyucking* hillbilly cousins in a Warner Bros. cartoon. After every long critical look, I'd pin my nose back with the bridge of my glasses and oink like a pig.

Like everyone else on the planet, I knew beauty had undeniable power. I'd seen how people reacted to my mother. I could have put together a whole album of pictures of her posing for Daddy's camera in her blue two-piece swimsuit. Her perfect skin looks so untouched by the sun it almost glares. Her lips are so big and her teeth so straight, every smile in the album looks come-hither. It's no wonder that in every single picture of her posing like that there's always one hapless sap caught in the margins staring at her as if his heart's about to go nova.

I craved that kind of clout, and since I now felt too ugly to get my bang from beauty and too old to start cramming to be a genius, there seemed to be only one path to supremacy left open to me. I had noticed that, ugly or not, idiots or not, boys always had an aura of authority, of primacy. Or that's how it looked from where I stood as a nine-and-a-half-year-old in 1960, when every official, from the president in D.C. to the second assistant mail clerk in Podunkum, was a man. Given my dearth of choices, I decided, during one of my self-mocking, self-loathing sessions in front of the mirror, to opt for the shrewdest survival tactic my nearly ten-year-old brain could imagine: I'd hunker down and seriously transform myself into a male.

From that day on, my sacred quest, like Pinocchio's, was to become a real boy. The minute I got home from school I'd change out of my navy polyester pleated skirt, my white rayon button-up blouse, and my pinchy black patent leathers into a pair of faded beige corduroys, a well-worn blue flannel shirt, and my precious red sneakers that were ratty as mother would allow. I kept my hair neither short nor long but a middling in-between, not unclean or neglected, just let be. I'd "forget" to wear my hearing aids and glasses, omissions that gave me a squinty little scowl and a reckless, unheeding air that made me seem tougher than I actually was. I fought with my more disreputable boy friends even when I didn't have to and cultivated the requisite foul mouth of a standard little thug. It helped that even deaf and half-blind (sans the hearing aid and glasses) I could still pitch a fastball that left most batters fuming.

But for all the vigor of my performance there'd still come a time during our games when the boys I yearned to emulate would split off and leave me behind. It wasn't until the beginning of summer, right after school let out, that I figured out the magic trick that would get me in thick with the gang of boys I sweated blood to join.

I'm not sure why I believed their gang of three had the power to convey boyness upon me. They were an unlikely-looking group of toughs. Charles Potter, the leader, had a buzz cut, but he was, on the whole, kind of plump for a bully. The other two were whey-faced blond brothers who both answered to "Hey, thief," and were that knotty kind of skinny I'd later come to associate with beer, knives, and a filmy look around the eyes. The three met informally and infrequently and didn't really have rules, just impulses. They'd launch into games of war, cowboys and Indians, and tag that always turned into wrestling fistfights. Most of their play was simply stupid, running around hitting each other. But when they were feeling bored and slightly imaginative they took it upon themselves to torment girls. It was this practice I recognized as my ticket to belonging.

Girls tended to like me, because I'd develop a crush on them if they simply said my name with a smile, and that made me seem pliant and sweet. They trusted me and my dumbstruck heart. It was a grave mistake. I might love the girls but I lusted for power. I tapped my softer feelings toward them only to hone my performance as the lure, the perfect bait. The boys and I would gather in the afternoon and circle the playground like scummy little hyenas, sizing up the girls as they jumped rope or dangled from the jungle bars. We'd keep to our side of the playground until we'd singled out the weakest one of the herd. Then it was time for me to get to work. I'd saunter across the invisible divide just like I belonged. Even though I could feel my own deception nibbling at my heart, it must never have shown, because I was always welcomed by those girls to join them at jump rope or hopscotch or drawing pictures in the dirt with a stick. Somewhere in the middle of our amiable play I'd ask the girl we'd chosen to please come talk to me privately. I was troubled and needed a friend's advice. These were nice girls, the ones whose hearts had been taught to melt at the mere mention of a friend in need. Their tenderness had once made me fond, but since hooking up with the boys, I'd come to regard it with a certain scorn, a weakness I could manipulate for my own greater good. If those girls hesitated even the slightest, I'd make my eyes well up and say, "Ah, dang. I left my hearing aids home. Can we talk someplace quiet?" I'd feed them that line and they'd follow me like baa-lambs to their doom.

Once I had lured the girl behind the Dumpster, the boys would jump out of hiding and help me throw her to the ground. Then one by one the boys would get on top of her, kiss her hard enough to wedge her mouth open, then let go with a dribble of spit. That was it. The third time we captured another weak one, the boys were taking their turns sitting on her, two of them kneeling on her arms while I sat on her feet. She was crying for help and her mother but her mouth was full of spit so it came out, "Haolbulb, haolbulb." We all thought that was pretty funny. Then the boys offered me a turn. Although I'd enjoyed the camaraderie up until then, I'd never been asked to mount the girl before. When they offered me my place in line I felt as honored as if I'd been asked to join the Marines. I could feel my body snapping to as if a just war had been

declared and the Stars and Stripes unfurled. I started suck-
ing on my cheeks to get the longest, most drooling piece
of spit among the bunch of us (it had become something of
a contest by then) and got on top of her. As I leaned in to
kiss her I made the mistake of looking her in the eyes, and
there it was—a look with which I was already too damned
familiar.

The family who lived to the side of us had two preteen
boys with muscular dystrophy. Tenley and I hadn't specifically been told to be kind to them but we were. For the
most part, anyway. Tenley was playmates with the youngest, Nicky, who at seven could still run fast enough, still
fling himself down and pick himself up so he wouldn't be
left too far behind during all the neighborhood games.
But his older brother, Mike, who just months earlier had
been running around like Nicky with the rest of us, was
coming to a halt. You could see it happening. When he'd
try to walk a little faster, his eleven-year-old body would
churn and grind like an unoiled machine. I didn't want to
be friends with him. The effort, the will it took for him
to simply lift his feet, was exhausting to witness. I'd only
pretend to include him in our play when in my mind
he really wasn't. The other kids must have taken my cue,
because when we forgot him during the chases or when
he never reappeared during hide-and-seek, no one asked
where he was or if he was coming. We just played right
over his tardiness, his absence.

Once, though, when I was leaping (freed of my hearing
aids and glasses) quick as a rabbit back and forth through
the *ratatattat* pulse of the sprinkler, I caught his expression.
He was in his swim trunks, and his body was as thin as you
can get without dying. The sight of him stopped me. Not

my body but the moment, in my soul. Because in his face I thought I saw a yearning. For a kind of mercy, maybe. As if he were giving in to some great wrong but still couldn't bring himself to relinquish hope. And I couldn't bear to see it. Couldn't bear knowing he would be denied.

So it was him (and myself in the mirror) I saw in the eyes of that girl the boys held pinned to the ground. I went ahead and did my duty—kissed her, spat. But that put period to me and the Potter gang.

The Performance
of Drowning

I OWE MIKE AND NICKY my single stint at the Texas Lions
Camp for Crippled Children. The beginning of summer
1960, my first summer as a disabled child, their mother
gave my mother a brochure extolling the virtues of a camp
in Kerrville, Texas, which my mother passed on to me. I
don't remember a single picture in the brochure. There
might not have been any. But I didn't need any help imagining myself riding horseback through the woods, hitting
the bull's-eye on an archery range, or slamming backhands
on a clay court in my tennis whites. Now that I think
back on it, I was probably channeling images from a tampon commercial. It hardly mattered. I was hot for summer
camp as only a child who has never been to camp can be.
And this camp was one my parents could afford, because
it was free to kids who were disabled, or, in the lexicon
of the time, crippled. I was delighted to discover that my
disabilities could actually yield a few dividends, even after
Mother explained to me that Lions Camp was a *special* one,
not quite like the camps she knew I was imagining. By the

coming fall, "special" would have grimmer connotations, but that summer I took the word to mean fun.

In the weeks before I boarded the transport van to camp, my mind was a sunny place to be, although in a dark, recessed corner of it I sat narrowing my eyes, plotting the many ways I'd avoid Mike and Nicky, who were going to camp, too. On the ride there I managed to avoid them the way I'd taken to avoiding anyone I didn't want to waste my time on. I pretended I couldn't hear them. Our whole journey though the scrubby hills of central Texas I sat with my face to the window, listening to the brothers as they talked together, their voices filtering through my hearing aids as tinny, intermittently comprehensible jabber. They were polite boys so I knew they would eventually try to involve me in their conversation, reach out and touch me to get my attention. When they did, I jumped as if they had sprinkled acid on my skin. "God almighty!" I squeaked, panting and holding my heart. "You mean to scare me half to death?" When they were good and contrite I turned magnanimous and deigned to listen, making them repeat whatever they had to say as many times as I could get away with. The repetition quickly tired the boys out, as I knew it would. They had to take a breather and leave our dialogue dangling, which allowed me to look sadly victimized and aggrieved, as if I suspected that their little *rest* really meant they had run out of patience with poor deaf me. I made sure they saw my eyes glisten and my mouth go slack with hurt before I turned back to the window and my own cheery self-enthrallment.

I was pretty sure I was going to be the one-eyed man in the country of the blind at this camp for cripples, and I couldn't wait to lord it over. My one week of camp would reveal me to be an expert horseback rider and a zing of an archer, like Maid Marian in *Robin Hood*. I'd turn lean as a whippet and brown as Kim and make friends with a midnight-blue stallion like Fury and together we'd watch over the populace, save a couple of lives, maybe Mike and Nicky, who could probably be counted on to end up lost in the brambles. There would be, I decided, no camper more gloriously worshipped than I.

Then the van pulled up to the Lions Camp for Crippled Children parking lot and we disembarked. I took one look around and every scheming thought in my head went *ffitt*. The asphalt was awash in a sea of bodies like none I had ever seen before—bodies that were gnarled into knots or had stumps instead of arms or plastic legs instead of real ones. There were bodies with eyes that were milk-white and unseeing, bodies that bucked in their wheeled chairs or drooled when they spoke. A couple of the bodies had a strange, unbalanced gait as if they were walking too fast on their tiptoes. Another had shoulders that sloped into boneless-looking flaps of flesh, like the flippers of a porpoise. And these were all the bodies of children, hundreds of them. I remember wondering, *Where in the hell did these guys come from?* They might as well have popped up from some Grimm brothers' underworld, the sight of them so unnerved me.

As the buses and cars and vans exited the grounds, the counselors rounded us up into one big herd, which they then divided by gender and age into smaller droves. I no longer had to worry about being stuck with Mike or Nicky, although from the minute we'd stepped off the van, I'd clung to them both. They went their way and I went mine as I was steered, along with eight other nine-to-eleven-year-old girls, to the Chippewa cabin. Of my eight fellow Chippewas I recall only three with any clarity. Dolores, paralyzed from the neck down, is most vibrant to my memory because she was my refuge during those first confused days of camp. She had the soft brown eyes of Bambi with a disposition to match, and I developed an instant and abiding crush on her. I remember the girl, if not her name, whose left leg had been crushed under a car, because the accident gave her an aura of tragic glamour. First thing in the morning and last at night a handful of us would huddle around her cot to watch her strap or unstrap the prosthesis to her nub. The blind girl (if not her name) sticks in my mind, in part because she was something of a prissy little snob but in larger part because she and One Leg were my chief foes during the daily swimming competitions held at the deep end of the camp pool.

My first day at camp I had been dismayed to discover that there was no archery, no tennis, and no horses, hence no horseback riding. There were crafts, and we were promised what I instantly surmised would be a mockery of camping out—we'd spend one night under the stars a good ten feet away from the cabins. The only thing the camp had in abundance, it seemed, was water. Besides a nice-sized creek (which we weren't allowed near) there was a huge pool divided into two halves, shallow and deep. At the shallow end were all the kids who were too physically disabled to swim alone. At the deep end were those of us who had lucked out. In our little cluster of Chippewas there were just three of us who were deep-enders—Blind Girl, One Leg, and me, Deafie. We had the muscle to lift up our heads, the coordination to get a forkful of food to our mouths, and the sensation to know when we had to shit or pee and enough physical control to hold it until we could. These skills marked us as separate from most of our peers.

For our mastery of these skills we were granted the boon of racing for half an hour, twice a day, each day, from one side of the deep pool to the other, using a variety of strokes taught to us by the deep-end instructor, an aqua-eyed, honey-haired goddess of the water. After each half-hour lesson, during the ten-minute free time before our races, she would join us in the pool via one of her perfect splashless dives. I don't know about Blind Girl, who was aloof and a bit imperious toward all of her Chippewa companions, but One Leg and I were enamored of the deep-end instructor and that tall, tan, accomplished body of hers. We two had adjoining cots and at night before we slept we'd mull over that body. The beauty of it as it knifed through the water, so unremarkable, so unmemorable, so very normal, with nothing to distinguish it but the grace with which it moved. Our hearts throbbed with her every stroke.

I remember no such heart throbbing for any of the shallow-end instructors. I suppose they were too busy to display their accomplishments or even to have any. It was their job to look out for all the other kids in the camp, the ones like my love, Dolores, who couldn't feed themselves, couldn't hold it, couldn't turn their heads or lift a finger. These guardians of the shallow end always worked in pairs, floating their charges in large lazy circles as they talked incessantly, encouraging the children, who were always made anxious by the water, to relax, to expand their lungs just a little more, just enough to pull in an extra bit of air. In our ten minutes of free swim time, I would wrap my arms around the bobbing barrier that separated deep from shallow, us from them, getting as close as I could to that other side. I was fascinated when one of the floaters, as we called them, would take in a breath with the same determined calculation of a bodybuilder preparing to lift a ton of dead weight; then, after a glance at the two smiling, nodding women who held her, she'd turn her face to the water and with that extra push of air create a ripple across the surface.

The effort those children put into the one small act of breathing made me uneasy. It frightened me to see them struggle so. *And for what?* That was the question unfolding in my mind then about the floaters (including my beloved Dolores), about crippled children generally, and, more alarmingly, about me and my two swimming rivals, even though we three were the favored.

Competition among the favored at the deep end of the pool was fierce and scored by results, not just effort. What determined those results were the daily races. My compatriots and I were already unquestioning little capitalists, well versed in the economy of winning. We knew whoever racked up the most daily races would collect the coveted, two-handled, gold-painted plastic cup with the word best lettered across its middle. But it was the unspoken dividend of scoring the trophy that inspired our most competitive extremes—the attention of the deep-end instructor herself. At the gala end of the summer awards ceremony we knew it would be she who would bend her pale-eyed gaze on the most deserving one of us, she who would pass that prize like a torch, she who would attest that here was one child, disabled though she might be, unarguably worth the effort it might take to keep her alive.

And that child was going to be me. I was sure of it, and not just because I was a strong swimmer and getting stronger. In my red, raw heart I felt destined to beat those other two out, because even though I'd lost my hearing, even though my mind sometimes still got lost in a whir of phantasmagoria, I had a talent they did not—I could pass for normal. That's what I had inadvertently been doing all those years before I was diagnosed. All I had to do was junk the glasses and hearing aids and adopt a supercilious air. In my mind that ugly little cup wouldn't just be confirmation of my superiority as a swimmer, it would be testimony to my essential ordinariness as a child. I simply had to win that thing.

Warming up in the water on the sixth day of camp, I felt cocky about my odds of eventually storing that trophy on my shelf. To my right was Blind Girl, who, always reckless despite the clueless texture of the water, had already twice bonked her head against the side of the pool. To her right was One Leg, who was, as usual, working ferociously to balance her lopsided weight so she wouldn't keep paddling in circles. I remember feeling a certain gleeful pity as I checked out the competition. I was sorry for their troubles but didn't mind that their woes had worked to my advantage, because up until that afternoon I had proved victorious in every race but two. I decided I could afford to be magnanimous in this last, less-than-crucial victory. I'd deliberately slow my pace and beat them by a half length instead of a full one.

Usually, at the start of our dash through the water, the deep-end instructor would stand at the opposite end of the pool in a vivid red bathing suit that, although a blur to my eyes, always got and held my attention. After a suspenseful pause, she'd chop her arm down like an ax while screeching, "Go!" The screech was for Blind Girl and the chop was for me.

On this particular day, though, we begged for the privilege of doing the ready-set-going among ourselves. First dibs went to One Leg, who, as an alluring amputee, was always accorded special status among those of us with more pedestrian disabilities. In addition to having lost a leg, she also had a mild speech impediment (which, as an aside, was in no way connected to the accident that had deprived her of her limb). I don't mean to suggest that her slurry speech cost me the race. Even if she had had the necessary crispness of enunciation, the fullness of volume, the perfectly modulated emphasis that would have left no doubt that when she said "gloah" she meant "go," it wouldn't have changed the outcome. Without my hearing aids, I couldn't hear in the water, and without my glasses, I couldn't see. Or rather I could only see what I had accustomed myself to seeing, and I was accustomed to seeing an unmistakable, if fuzzy, sweeping chop of air when all I was getting this time was a tiny, slurring blur of lips. I knew that somewhere within that miniblur was just a simple "Ready, Set, Go!" but I couldn't quite bring myself to trust my own crude perception. I felt befuddled by my insecurity, afraid that if I'd read her lips wrong and she was saying something unexpected, like "Very wet toes," I'd start too soon and look like I was cheating to get an even more unfair advantage. All of which was why I kept my grip on the side of the pool after "gloah" had been duly pronounced. And in those long seconds of hesitation, both my rivals shot out an unbeatable span in front of me.

It took another second of confusion before I had the

wherewithal to loosen my hold and start paddling furiously after them, but by then the race was lost and I knew it. Now this needn't have been a particularly humiliating failure. I had already racked up the wins I needed to be best and the two other times Blind Girl had beaten me I'd been able to shrug it off. I'd been distracted at the start of my first defeat, busy squinting my eyes at the shallow end, trying to pinpoint my Bambi-eyed love Dolores so I could wave. My second loss, I just felt too lazy to really try. But on this afternoon, my day had been a long one. I was homesick and lonely, and at breakfast Dolores and I had a tiff because I didn't think she was paying me enough attention. Then at crafts, before lunch, I'd deliberately shattered the clay ashtray I'd made for my mother because to my critical eye it didn't look enough like a rattlesnake coiling. In the canteen at noon, I had sat munching my PB&J, brooding over fickle love and artistic failure and bitterly berating myself for even being at this sorry excuse for a camp. Camp was supposed to be the place where I'd finally come into my own, shed the fleshy misinterpretation of my soul and gradually be transformed back into the conquering good-looker I knew I was meant to be. And it wasn't happening. It was only after I had changed into my swimsuit, jumped into the pool, and started practicing the Australian crawl that my gloom began to lift. Just being around the deep-end instructor made me feel tingly with hope, and by the time we'd finished our lesson and were ready to race, I was just about in love with life again. Then, ready, set, poof! There I was once more—my own tubby, ill-favored little self in a messy competition with two other cripples who were going to beat *me* in a pathetic water race for a plastic two-handled cup.

I wanted to stop the action, demand that we start over again because I hadn't heard the right words. I'd been fouled by my deafness and that's why I wasn't going to win and it just wasn't fair. I knew how my two competitors would react to that, the same way I would have— with scorn. Blind Girl wouldn't bother or maybe wouldn't even know how to hide her visible contempt, and One Leg would swirl her stump around in the water and flick a look over at the shallow end of the pool, a reminder, like her stump, that far greater, far more visible tragedies than mine existed. I knew that no matter what excuse I offered up for losing, there'd be no excuse, not even to my own mind, really. Even when I wore the glasses and hearing aids that made my own flaws visible, I knew that among those other disabled kids at camp I could never be handicapped enough. Which made it all the more humiliating that my own modest disabilities had tripped me up, made a fool of me. A loser, I thought, to losers.

All my life I had felt as if there were an eye on me, not necessarily a hostile eye but a feared one, like an eye of God or an eye of the world, as if the very substance of the air were judging if I were fit to live, fit to be loved. Where I got that feeling I didn't know, but I always imagined the eye as either kinder than my grandma or meaner than me at my meanest. That day at the pool, I felt as if the cruelest of eyes was fixed on me as I flailed in the water, looking on me the way I looked on the floaters. In the context of a good, hard race, they were a joke. It didn't matter that they were working just as hard, maybe harder than I would ever work in my life, for the dubious pleasure of blowing a few fucking bubbles in the water. I knew the eye that fastened on me would never call that winning. I had already felt its cold, unforgiving gaze once before at this camp, on the first day we had lined up for lunch when I had tried not to stare in distaste at the kids around me but couldn't quell the angry thought bubbling up from nowhere that they ought to be kept out of sight. Then my skin prickled and my stomach dropped when I realized I'd meant me, too. Floundering there in the pool, I wasn't articulating it like this. I was just a child. I was simply feeling it all as a shamed, whirling loss of heart that was threatening to overwhelm me. So I took the only action I could think against that sea of troubles. I drowned.

Forcing yourself to drown, willing yourself to sink, isn't as easy a thing to do as you might imagine. But I did it. I sank a little, dropped an inch or so under the water until my natural buoyancy bobbed me right back up. The deep-end instructor saw me go under. I could feel her eyes on me the moment I decided to let go, and as I slipped under the surface a second time, I felt a thrill of real panic because I knew with that double dip my bit of fakery had just gotten out of hand. We were a camp for crippled kids, so everything that surrounded us was viewed as a potential danger. Many of the kids needed the simplest things just to keep them alive and breathing. In a place like that there could be no false alarms, because a kid who just seemed to be coughing a bit too long and hard might very well be choking on his own mucus. Any small thing gone wrong might be a harbinger, the beginning of a real tragedy that could exist because such tragedies actually did exist. As far as the camp counselors were concerned, a cry for help was always and only the real thing. I was going to be rescued whether I deserved it or not. I'd given myself no choice but to choke, flail, and carry out my drowning to its frothy, chest-compressed end. And it was a first-rate, compelling enactment, if I do say so myself.

I knew the superficialities of drowning from TV, how the body is snatched down, then shoots up again, spluttering. In cartoons, the nails of Wile E. Coyote's paw ping up through the water, one, two, and then three before he waves bye-bye and sinks to the bottom of a lake. But I knew a bona fide drowning wouldn't be quite that simple. The real act of drowning, as I had learned from the kids at the shallow end, was all about the deprivation of air. Spying on the floaters had taught me how to make my fight for breath seem desperate and real. I knew from watching their daily struggles how to mimic their fear that their last suck, their last gasp, might be the one they had just taken. And from my own feelings of despair that were threatening to overwhelm me there in the water, I knew how to give up, give in, be perfectly drawn down. As I slipped under the water for a third time, I gulped in great gouts of liquid, so when I bubbled up again I was choking and spewing, as if the pathetic victim I was making of myself had tragically mistaken the killing element of water for the saving grace of air. I came as close to drowning as I possibly could to make my act ring true, look real, be worthy of rescue. I was so perfectly convincing that my audience was taken in, Blind Girl, One Leg, shallow-enders all—the actions of their lives were brought to a halt by my performance of drowning.

It was then that the deep-end instructor unwittingly joined me in my act, diving in to play out her own role of savior. She cut through the churning water and reached down to lift my head up to face the blue sky, and then with perfect strokes (exactly as she'd rehearsed every day of her lifeguard training) she pulled me away from the beckoning depths and hauled my ass out of the water. On the hot concrete where she laid me, we made an elegant duo. She'd push my chest and I'd let the watery froth come rolling out of my mouth as if it had been lodged in my lungs rather than merely held at the back of my throat. When finally I thought the timing right, I gagged, spluttered, opened my eyes, and she, looking into that perfectly mimicked gaze of someone who had eyeballed death by water, pulled me to her as I shivered and wept, and held me tight against the wet, panting, perfect body that I loved.

So I was saved. It was such a sincere, driven act of rescue, with such an excruciatingly sexual culmination, I could hardly bear the shame of knowing I'd only been acting. I feared the universe was bound to make me pay dearly for my theatrics, if only because I had enjoyed them so much. Even as the counselors were toweling my shaking body dry, I was privately reveling over how deliciously I had fooled everyone with my marvelous acting technique, with its attention to detail. The rest of the afternoon I kept expecting a bolt from the blue to knock my fraudulent soul flat. But that day passed, and then another, without the slightest grumble of thunder, and I began to believe myself safe from divine retribution. Then, on the last evening of camp, came Awards Night.

I'm not sure what I expected from Awards Night, but early on, Dolores and I (who had by then reconciled) realized there were prizes for both real and, shall we say, fictitious accomplishments. By the time the camper with cerebral palsy, whom we all knew to be a fatuous brownnoser, was given Most Cheerful, the jig was definitely up. I couldn't help but flinch when the girl in the wheelchair next to me grabbed the halter that held the big box speaker of my hearing aid and yelled, "You won Best Swimmer!" I was acutely aware that I wasn't the popular choice among the other kids at camp. I also knew my peers, in their disgruntlement with the outcome, would be inclined to view my winning as the Almost Drowned sympathy vote. I had to think fast. I was desperate for the majority's good opinion, which had eluded me up to then, possibly because during our week together I had inadvertently committed a string of faux pas—calling the dwarf, who was a year my elder, a little cutie, doing a Jerry Lewis silly walk that looked exactly like the gait of the unctuous twerp with cerebral palsy, and grabbing Blind Girl (who hated to be touched) by the arm to pull her along because she was, as I explained when she got all hissy, holding up the line. Every other attempt I'd made at friendship—with the exceptions of Dolores and One Leg—seemed to fall flat. I couldn't figure out why. I imagined all those other kids as some-how belonging to each other, all of them part of a tight group, knit close as family. It had come to seem cozy and safe and I thought if only I could awaken that kind of love in them, they'd give me a break, realize that even though I might look as if I'd got off scot-free, I still had my own suffering to attend. I think I was groping for some quick, graphic shorthand to demonstrate how closely we actually were akin, that I meant well and longed to be one of their number. That's the only reason I can think of for what I did next. I limped all the way up to the stage on one leg and all the way back on the other. Thankfully, the only one who seemed to have noticed my tilting hobble was Dolo-res, who asked me if I had twisted my ankle. I lied and said "Yeah, both of them."

Two hours later, when everyone else was abed, I lay awake on my cot, feeling vaguely like a martyred saint and kind of liking it. It had dawned on me that while I might not ever be universally beloved, I was taking home the real prize and it wasn't a chintzy bit of plastic. The deep-end instructor had grabbed *me,* pulled *my* body to hers, wept over *me.* Those were *my* lips she had pressed her own against, *my* dripping body she had dried off with a towel. I'd been publicly intimate with the woman, for God's sake, and art, not competitiveness, had earned me her divine embrace. A single dramatic performance had got me miles beyond any old dinky swimming award. I chafed for a bubble gum cigarette as I mulled over my ill-got knowledge—how drama trumps the day-to-day, how easily pity can be milked and love manipulated, how the false, when perfectly enacted, can be even more poignant than the true. It seemed seriously adult to know these things, more serious than a children's camp could allow. But even as I lay there, staring with a certain smugness at the nothing that was the ceiling, I could feel my punishment taking shape in the back corner of my heart.

Once when I was five and on my way home from school, I'd fixed my white cotton sweater to look like a sling and told the bus driver that I'd broken my arm. He'd known I was lying and his sorrowful eyes had made me feel like the most wicked of deceivers. That trifling deception had haunted me for years, and this latest ruse seemed a much more serious breach. I thought about getting up from my bunk, tiptoeing down the hall to the deep-end instructor's room to knock at her door and tell her the facts. I knew if I did knock and she opened her door I'd probably just stand there mutely beseeching and let the tortured expression in my eyes pass for the truth. But if, as I feared and longed, she actually invited me into her room or, dare I imagine it, took me under her covers to stroke my back until I slept or just passed out from the sexual tension—or even if she just simply invited me into her room—I knew I'd break down. Confide in her that none of what had so intimately passed between us in those spine-tingling moments of rescue had been remotely real, confess that the award she had so innocently presented to me was not for Best Swimmer but Best Actress. And those were secrets I couldn't bring myself to share. It seemed wiser to opt for sleep, which I did, curling my exultant, shame-racked body in a ball.

Lost Boy

I WAS ALWAYS A CHILD who hated goodbyes. I'd got it
into my deaf little head that the minute I could no longer see or touch the people I loved, they ceased to be. After every holiday visit to my mother's family, it took me
forever to make my farewells. I'd cling like a possum to
my grandma, my grandpa, my aunt, my uncles, my aunts-
by-marriage, my hundreds of cousins, all in turn, kissing
them repeatedly while shedding buckets of tears, carrying
on as if I knew the minute our car pulled out of the gravel
driveway the whole lot of them and the house they were in
would blow sky high then sink right through the ground.
I never had the grace to be embarrassed by my own lack
of forbearance, and even now as an adult I cry and cling,
although I don't make the people I'm leaving feel as if I
know something they don't about the span of their lives.
I may have learned how to pull in the reins of sorrow somewhat, but I still find that people cease to exist for me when
they're out of my range of sight. I'm in Texas now, visiting my mother, and I suspect, just knowing the morning
routine of this visit, that she's downstairs in the kitchen

chatting with my sisters. But I can't hear them, and my body feels no evidence of their presence, not a trembling of the air, not a prickling of my skin. It's like the crickets and birds that everyone tells me are chittering and whistling in the grass and trees. I'm enchanted by the thought, but my body feels no trace of those sounds being there, surrounding me. I have often thought that it is that inbuilt quietus that makes all my goodbyes feel the same, with "Good night," being as emotionally fraught as "Someone just died," or "I never want to see you again."

That may be why I am disturbed that I don't remember my summer-camp farewells. I would have imagined, given my nature, they'd be seared to my brain, but I have no recollection of pressing my forehead against Dolores's hair or kissing her ear or huddling with the other Chippewas, sobbing promises to write. I think, instead, that I hid, gathered the soft bag that held my laundry-marked navy shorts and white, snap-front short-sleeved shirts, and, in the flurry of packing, slipped out of the cabin to wait on one of the picnic tables for my family to come rescue me. I do remember that when finally they arrived to pick me up for the drive to Jacksboro and our summer visit to my grandparents, I went running to them as fast as I could, faster than any other child at camp, and leapt and danced in front of the car when it came to a halt.

Once on the road, I flaunted my trophy but kept the commentary to a minimum. I keep thinking, now, that I must have at least told them about the floater who, whenever she got good and mad, snapped her teeth, trying to bite anybody within chomping range. But my family says no, they don't remember me saying a thing about my week at camp. I was almost ten by then and maybe that's not a confiding age. Or perhaps I didn't yet have the language to explain what had happened, all I had witnessed. Whether I had the words or not, I had the lucidity to know there had been changes worked on my soul and that they weren't particularly good ones. They didn't, for instance, make me more adult or kind.

Our summer visit to Jacksboro marked the first time my mother's family would see me decked out in my new gadgetry. On Wednesday of that week, my Granny Doris hauled me to a faith healer during a revival at her Free Holiness church. I knew it was meanness to get up there to be healed, to stand in line with all the sincerely hopeful, to let the Brother put his hand on my brow exhorting God to have mercy on his sad little lamb, to act dazzled and cured, throw my glasses to the floor and shout, "I can see! I can walk!" then bump into the wall and tumble to the floor. Even after the Brother kneeled down, smiling, and offered me a hand up, I couldn't manage to feel ashamed.

I was being eaten up by an anger akin to grief, and while I found some solace in half-assed tricks, I was desperate to get my old body back, the one I'd been so enamored of, the unencumbered body that would grow up, I kept fighting to believe, into my ideal version of it—a smiling, good-looking son of the West. Like Roy Rogers or the Cunningham men, my mother's father and brothers. My mother had seven brothers and one lone sister, Sue. We girls loved our Aunt Sue, a chatty, skinny redhead who topped my mother by a foot even though she was twelve years younger. But we reserved our crushes for Kenny, Jerry, and Jimmy, the three of the seven uncles who were still at home when we were growing up. They were all handsome, sweet-smelling boys who wore the boots, the jeans, the fresh-pressed white shirts and shade-brimmed hats of cowboys. Like their father, they wore Brylcreem on their hair and Old Spice on their cheeks, and they loved to charm and tease us three Galloway girls.

From the first day I ever remember laying eyes on them, when I was five and we were visiting from Germany, I coveted their Texas mystique. I'd stick Kenny's hat on my head, Jerry's boots on my feet, and borrow Jimmy's ukulele (which I thought was a guitar), and clomp around the house, strumming notes at random, yodeling tone-deaf renditions of "How Much Is That Doggie in the Window?" The boys thought my impromptu performances were funny, and sometimes when I'd deck myself out they'd pat my cheeks with a dab of aftershave. As good-humored as they were about me taking possession of their hats, shoes, and musical instruments, they wouldn't let me touch their .22s, which I had discovered while rummaging through the clothes in their closets.

Rifles and the whole idea of shooting one became a kind of obsession for me, and after we had settled back in Texas I started pestering my uncles to let me go on one of their nighttime rabbit kills. It wasn't until the Lions Camp summer, when I appealed to them in my new persona as a piteous, handicapped waif, that they finally let me tag along, although my parents scotched any fantasy I had of handling a firearm. On the big night, my Grandpa Chuck did the driving, gunning his pickup over the grassy dirt, lights on high beam. Trudy and I were in the front seat with him, while the boys stood on the running board or leaned out from the bed of the truck. I remember seeing what must have been a warren of rabbits scattered over the field. The rabbits that were caught dead center in the glare of the headlights froze in terror, and my mind froze with them. Then a bullet hit one, kicked it into the air and made it squeal. The truck kept right on moving and the boys kept shooting till there was nothing left to shoot. Then Grandpa circled around, drove back slowly over the field of slaughter, the boys walking by the side of the truck gathering up the bodies. I didn't know what to make of it when Kenny gave me a plump-bellied rabbit to hold. I would have cradled it in my lap like a cat but it was oozing viscera, so he showed me the right way to do it—by its hind legs, at arm's length.

Back at the house there were two big kettles of water at a boil. Our grandmother did the disemboweling over a bowl in the sink. I remember standing in the doorway watching her slit the belly of the rabbit I'd held. As its young fell into the bowl sack by sack with wet little plops I thought I saw the membranes kick, as if they were struggling to escape. And when my grandmother sliced the tissues open with her knife and tipped the bodies—which I was sure were still alive—into the boiling water, I wanted to run into the other room and bury my face in my daddy's arms. But I willed myself to stand there, to attend. I thought there must be something in this ritual of slaughter I was bound to witness if I were ever going to become the man I was determined to be, the square-jawed westerner with a stomach for that kind of killing. Like my Grandpa Chuck.

My grandfather was a short, barrel-chested, cleft-chinned man's man who was feared for his temper but who would let us girls comb his hair like a woman's and do up his face with our mother's makeup. We'd pluck his eyebrows, pick over his back, and examine the stumps of his left hand where all four fingers and the thumb had been cut off at the knuckles. Grandfather's stumps were a source of fascination to all his grandchildren, and we'd urge him to treat us to a show of lighting his cigarettes with a match. He'd use his abbreviated thumb to hold down the matchbook, pinch off a match with the stumps of his index and second fingers, and then strike hard till it flared. He called that hand his "paw," and we children were as fond of it as if it were a favorite pet. His grandkids liked to surprise him in his field office, a tin shed just across the red clay earth of the yard from the house. The shed smelled of unfiltered Camels, Old Spice, and the sweet musky leather of his work boots and gloves. There he taught us how to shuffle and deal cards, play poker, and keep down the little nips of whiskey we'd sip from the bottle he kept in his desk drawer. Pinups of Marilyn Monroe were on his office wall along with feed calendars, work sheets, and newspaper clippings detailing the football heroics of his sons. He had been a rough father to his children, but it was to him I looked for stories of sweet redemption, where the scars on a body are the marks of honor and a tragic hurt turns out to be a saving grace.

When Grandpa Chuck was a young man, he'd been a roughneck searching for oil in the flatlands of northwest Texas. They were called roughnecks because the back of their necks would tan to a kind of bumpy leather as they worked the rigs under the sun. Those old oil drills, so Grandpa told us, had steel coils wrapped around their shafts to make them bite the earth deeper. Sometimes the drill would hit a massive chunk of rock that would jar it to a cracking halt. When that happened, the coil would snap from its fastenings and come whipping up out of the ground with a distinctive *whup whup whupping* sound, like a flat steel blade spinning through the air. To the regular crew, who knew that the whirling coil of steel would cut through anything, flesh or metal, in its path, that sound was as familiar as the rattle of a snake.

According to this story of Grandpa's, Mr. Boaz of Boaz Oil had sent his only son to the Number Ten field to get some hands-on experience. The boy told the crew boss he'd worked a drill before, so no one thought to tell him about that sound, so familiar, or what it signified. It was getting on quitting time when the coil snapped and went whipping up. My grandfather said he saw the boy leaning over the lip of the hole like he was trying to see where all the commotion was coming from, and for a split second, Grandpa thought about leaving the fool to die. Instead, he leapt up onto the platform, pushed the boy to the planks, and was in the act of ducking down himself when the cable reared and struck. He threw his arm up to keep the steel off his neck, and when he did, it sliced clean through the four fingers and thumb of his left hand. The back part of his glove was still intact, so they let it be and drove him to the clinic. When the doctor pulled the glove off, the fingers went with it, all four and the top of the thumb. They didn't have the means then to put his hand back together, so that was that.

The first time I heard this story I patted Grandpa's ruined hand gingerly, feeling the same awe and admiration for it as I did for the tough old one-eared tom named Boots after he'd battled the roaming junkyard dog and won. You could see from Grandpa's right hand how pretty his left had once been. His mother, Eve, and her twin, Eve, who had the same shapely hands, were accomplished pianists, with Aunty being the better—as a young woman she periodically traveled from Philadelphia to Toronto to play with the philharmonic there. But even Grandfather's right hand wasn't unscathed and had a puckered scar in its palm from some accident he'd been in when he was twelve. The wound had gone right to the bone, and when it healed it left a deep half-moon that didn't get any shallower as he aged. I don't have any more details, because the accident itself was always made incidental to the rest of the story.

When he was a skinny sixteen-year-old and had snuck away from home to join the army and fight in the Great War, he was stationed on a base in coastal North Carolina. There he quickly fleshed out into a man. He was a good soldier, so good that, young as he was, he was promoted to stateside drill sergeant. One winter day, a platoon he was training received orders to ship out for the European front that very night. The hour before they were to embark, one of the enlisted men came to my grandfather's tent in a panic. He was a boy, even younger than my grandfather, and he'd lost his dog tags and had no idea where. Military law at the time decreed that any soldier found on the front without his tags was guilty of a crime punishable by death or imprisonment. My grandfather, who was stationed stateside for the duration of the fighting, took his own tags off and draped them around the boy's neck. The boy landed on a mine the minute he put a foot on European soil and there wasn't much left of him but those bogus tags. That's how my grandfather, Charles Llewellyn Cunningham, came to be reported as killed in action.

When Chuck's mother Eve received the telegram telling her that her son had died, she hadn't seen or heard from him in two years. I don't remember or maybe it was never said how long thereafter she lived with the news that she'd lost her son. When the war ended, my grandfather headed home, and on a late summer evening walked up to his parents' house and knocked. His mother opened the door and looked at him inquiringly. He was taken aback that she hadn't recognized him. He said, "Don't you know me?" She replied, "No, I don't believe we've ever been introduced." He said, "Mother, it's Charles." She wouldn't accept it. She still had the telegram informing her of his death folded in her Bible, and the man standing in front of her didn't look anything like the boy she had known. She said, "My son is dead."

I always thought it would have been instinctive for him to hold out the scarred palm as a shortcut through all the birth dates, the nicknames, the lists, the proofs, but my Grandpa said no, he didn't even think to show it. It was his mother who lifted up his hand and knew him instantly by that scar.

Those two weeks in Jacksboro I asked to be told the-boss's-idiot-son and the scar-on-the-palm stories whenever Grandpa was in a talkative mood. If he wasn't of a mind or if he was working, I'd pester my mother until she would tell them. I needed to hear those two stories again and again, the way I had once needed to hear *The Little Engine That Could*. It seemed of great consequence that his scar made him recognizable, that the rightful evidence of his heroic heart was his mangled fingers. With every retelling, I'd think maybe I still had a chance, maybe all my scarred and damaged friends at camp still had a chance to become the ones who rescue, sacrifice, blaze the path, save the day. I knew I'd never be able to save anyone if I couldn't hear a cable come whipping up, but these small bits of family history helped me believe I had it in me to find a way, be led by instinct or some other deep knowing, even if my own caustic heart was jeering it knew better.

Right next to our grandfather's office there was a fenced-in acre where the Boaz Oil Company kept its rigs, rock augers, drive motors, and hauling trucks. The lot was grassless, just gravel and hard-packed clay bordered by strands of barbed wire. I'd put my foot on the middle strand of wire, lift the top one, and ease my body through. I'd weave among the machines, their gas/oil smells a comfort, reminding me, like the tang of cigarettes, of my grandfather. When I had walked deep enough into that maze of engines, I'd kick the biggest tire of the biggest hauling truck and curse heaven and earth for doing such terrible wrong to me and my friends.

I didn't think anyone, much less my grandmother, suspected that bitter heart of mine. She was a woman kept busy by her family and her church. When I was nine she still had those three sons and a daughter at home. My mother sometimes complained that her mother spoiled those four, especially the boys. Granny Doris did everything for them, even ironed their jeans, my mother said. And it was true, she did, and still made time to play piano every Wednesday and Sunday at the Free Holiness church, singing rousing hymns in her clear, pretty voice. As a young woman she'd been the daughter of a Baptist minister, proper in her churchgoing. After her baby Robert died, she turned, for many years, to the charismatics, who, while they didn't go so far as to handle snakes, spoke in feverish tongues and believed in the healing power of their faith. Maybe I shouldn't have been so surprised, then, that it was she, more than anyone, who sensed the turbulence of my soul.

One morning as she hung wash, me at her elbow handing her the clothespins, she slapped a wet shirt on the line, then stopped as if she'd had a thought. She squatted down to be face-to-face with me so I could see her lips. "Honey," she said, "don't you be afraid. God has something special planned for you." My wizened little heart was hissing, *Yes, he plans to make me deaf.* But I just kissed the corner of her lips and said, "I love you too."

A week later, back home again in Fort Hood, I woke up from what had become a recurring nightmare——my mother hurrying past me on a busy street as if I were invisible. I'd call out to her, to let her know that it was me, that I was near, but even though I thought I was shouting, my voice was far too soft for her to hear. Before I could figure out the problem, she'd disappear.

I lay there for a long time pondering in the dark while everyone else in the house slept on. Then I made up my mind. Leaving my glasses and my hearing aids on the nightstand, I slipped out of bed. I pulled my jeans on, pushed my feet into the sneakers I never unlaced. From under the mattress, where I'd hidden them, I dug out the army shirt of my dad's I'd filched from the laundry room that morning, and the knotted tie I'd stolen from his closet the day before. Holding them in one hand, I snuck through the living room, where I stood for a moment to get my breath. My mother's lighter and cigarettes were on the coffee table, so I shoved them in my front pocket and made my way to the side door leading to the carport. I buttoned the shirt, slipped the tie over my neck. The shirt, tucked into my jeans, gave me a gratifying paunch. I felt prepared. That night (as on many nights after), I was on a mission. I'd patrol the streets of our little subdivision of the Fort Hood army base and keep things safe. And while I was at it, I just might stumble upon danger and romance. I was, after all, in the proper guise for encountering them. As I opened the door and stepped out at 3 a.m., I figured I'd start my three-block beat at the school playground, move on to the Officer's Club swimming pool, then swing around to check on the Quonset-hut library before sneaking back to bed. I straightened my tie, dug out a cigarette, lit it up, and stood there, my feet set wide apart, my paunch a kind of shield. I imagined I was the spitting image of my grandfather as he watched over the oil fields. I blew smoke through my nose as if I'd done it a hundred times instead of just that once, then started my rounds. I was halfway down the driveway when I took the chance I feared, looked straight up into the blur of stars, shook my fist, and hissed at the great *them* above me, "Just you try!" Nothing paid me the slightest mind. I suddenly felt as jaunty as a clever cartoon pig that has just outwitted a wolf. I was only a little girl playing dress-up at night, but I knew then that I had it in me to be a man. I had looked the intimidating bully of the universe right in the eye and stared it down, if only for a few uneasy seconds. If that were true, that I could be as fearlessly arrogant as my cowboy idols, as recklessly resolute and bold, then I knew those stars were as much mine as anyone's. I had a real shot at becoming, at the very least, the hero of my own story.

PART II

Passing

Little-*d* Deaf

I RECENTLY READ THAT hearing is the last of the senses to go. I've taken this to mean I'm going to be buried alive, because, deaf as I am, I won't know I'm not already dead. This alarming new bit of information moved me to take up the nonhearing exercises I used to indulge in when I was younger. I put my hearing aids aside, stretch out on the bed, and get myself ready for what's in store. The mattress trembles with every passing car and so do I. When a train rumbles and chugs along the tracks three blocks to the north, my body rumbles and chugs right along with it. Thunder shakes the walls of the little house where I live and the shocks of it make the headboard and my own heart thwack. Lying there awake too long breeds in me a deep unease, a fear that I ought to be feeling something I'm not. My longtime love, Donna Marie, calling for help in the back room; our cat, Tweety, yowling piteously to be let in. Those are the times when going deaf the way I have, in fits and starts, seems most akin to dying. I'm losing, will lose, have lost. And each step of the way, my body seems to have been trying to tell me something new, something it seems I ought to have known all along.

In 1961, the year after I was diagnosed, my body reached a tipping point and I began to lose my hearing in big old chunks. It was a loss as erratic and unsettling as a Ukrainian train schedule. I'd lose a decibel or two of sound, then my hearing would stabilize. A day, a week, a month later, whole conversations would fade into gibberish. Familiar noises like the purr of the refrigerator would simply vanish and I'd have to adjust all over again. One late afternoon I fell into a doze on the couch listening to my parents' muttered lazy Sunday conversation, then woke a handful of minutes later to what seemed like nothing. For two days even my own voice was an echo in my head.

I loved the crispness of my own speech, a trait both Trudy and I picked up from our German maids. When we first moved from Germany to Texas my precise enunciation marked me as somehow superior to those who drawled or squeezed words through their noses. After my deafness took hold, my speech began changing, every vowel out of my mouth taking on a soft slur that people took for southern. I didn't love the South then, the way I love it now. And that change to my voice embarrassed me, but not as much as it did to see the new incongruities of my voice reflected in people's faces, the wince when I was talking too loudly, the grimace when I wasn't talking loudly enough, or the skeptical twist of brow when I'd swear I didn't mean my tone to be angry, that I had no idea I sounded sardonic when I'd meant to sound sincere. I could feel all the lilt and color draining from my voice, feel it becoming a monotonous drone. I'd forget to give the end of a sentence a vocal twist to make it mean this one thing, or drop the sound in the middle to make it mean another. I found it hard to remember how words I knew sounded, harder still to learn new words I couldn't quite hear. My two sisters loved playing teacher, and made exaggerated facial displays, showing me how my lips should move to form the new syllables. But even with my new hearing aids it was hard to piece the muted gabble of sounds together into any kind of sense.

Hearing aids or no, I was constantly being taken unawares, and that made me jumpy, almost paranoid. I didn't realize someone was running around the corner until the body was upon me, didn't answer the voice calling from the bathroom until they'd got up off the toilet to scream, didn't know anyone was pounding at a locked door unless I accidentally opened it and they came tumbling through. I was a private child, made even more private by the confusion and intensity of my sexual desires, and everyone seemed to be sneaking up on me. I needed a big hunk of uninterrupted solitude to play out my needs to their natural conclusions, and it divided my focus having to keep one eye on my closed bedroom door and the other on my Barbie and Midge dolls having sex.

At the same time, I was discovering, to my repeated embarrassment, the Freudian element in lip reading. One memorable afternoon as I was inching forward in the lunch line, I looked up at the lips of the fourth-grade sex bomb who had just cut in front of me, and was wonderfully taken aback when she deigned to address me: "Hey kid, you've just made my day!" My heart started thumping like a happy Disney bunny until her flat inflection, her narrowed eyes, and the pinchy look around her nose clued me in to what she'd really just said, which was, "Hey pig, get out of my way." Who knew deafness could be so ironic?

All my mother and father knew of deafness was what they'd seen in a film called *Johnny Belinda,* about the rape of a tragically clueless deaf and mute girl doomed, like me, always to be taken by unwelcome surprise. All they knew about the deaf was that they signed. My parents didn't know what to think of Sign. They knew it to be a real language, but it was an alien one, something neither one of them—even my father, with his spy's proficiency in German and Russian—could ever imagine learning. When the Texas school system offered them the choice of leaving me in public school or enrolling me in a school for the deaf, they had no idea how to choose, and left it up to me. I'd seen only one person sign before, and the symbols her hands carved out of air seemed akin to the soundless language of the TV Apaches I so admired. I was already using my hands anyway—to gesture, touch, and feel. Sound was quickly seeping away from me, leaving me in a void I was anxious to fill. I would have welcomed that new way to understand. But for my mother's sake I wanted to appear whole again. I already knew how to do that—act cool and pretend all was well. Over pancakes one Sunday morning, my parents asked me if I wanted to transfer to a special school where they'd teach me to sign. I didn't even bother to think about it, just downed my cocoa and rolled my eyes as if they'd told the biggest joke in the world. "Sign? Hah. Not for me, thank you. And pass the syrup, please."

At public school in Fort Hood, I sat up front and did the best I could to learn, and each afternoon served out a two-hour sentence in the gulag known as special ed. Special ed was usually held in a one-room annex that looked like a trailer on stilts. There was a steep ramp with handrails running from the ground to the door. The room was dark and close and stuffy, just big enough to hold the handful of us special kids. There was usually someone in a wheelchair, someone blind, someone dull and thuggish, and at one point a sister and brother who seemed old to be in elementary school—they both had a shadow of a beard and a look about their eyes that reminded me of dogs turned mean after being poked at, beaten, and teased. I realize now they were probably mildly retarded, because whenever they talked, which was seldom, their faces would contort in rubbery exaggeration, as if they had to fight their own muscles to get the words out right. We did nothing productive those two hours we were together. Zero. Zilch. We sat, fidgeted, or stretched out and whiled away the hours. Since I was able-bodied I helped empty the pee bags and sometimes I'd read aloud while the volunteer assistant, whose Texas twang thrummed like an overtightened string, would correct my pronunciation, teaching me to say "fir" instead of "for" and "enny" instead of "any."

I was a clever little schemer and a voracious reader, so I managed to keep up in my regular classes at school, getting hard-won B's and A's even though the teachers had a bad habit of turning their backs as they were speaking to write on the blackboard. I'd read their lips as they said, "We call the theory that there is only one . . ." then they'd turn their backs and the rest would be lost in puffs of chalk. It didn't occur to me to ask my teachers to change their behavior, to look at me when they were talking, to slow down so I could read their lips. I was a child and thought I had no agency. But I knew I was flying by the seat of my pants, that every answer I gave was guesswork, that I couldn't really spell or diagram a sentence; and at age ten, then eleven, then twelve, I was still using my fingers to add and subtract. It wasn't until years later that I found out I'd been one of the lucky ones.

As a child I didn't pay much heed to other deaf children, because I didn't know any. The deaf as a people don't regard themselves as disabled but simply a culture entire, like the Amish. And, like the Amish, they keep to themselves. There is a definite hierarchy in that deaf culture. If you are deaf of deaf—a deaf person born to deaf parents—and your language is Sign and the company you keep is primarily deaf, you are Deaf with a capital *D*. If you are hearing-born to deaf and you sign and live and play primarily within the deaf community, your blood is still pure. It dilutes a bit with every variation from those first golden means, but lowest on the deaf totem pole are the waverers like me who came to deafness gradually or late and were "mainstreamed" to be part of the hearing world. As a general rule we suck at Sign. My own Sign is on par with my Spanish, which can get me to the bathroom, but after that, nada. We are known as the little-*d* deaf.

Growing up, I knew none of this. I was twenty-five before I went to my first deaf gathering, and I was taken aback to encounter hostility and suspicion there. When I introduced myself as Deaf, overenunciating and gesturing broadly with my hands, one of the women signed to me furiously, her eyes getting harder by the second as she realized how little I understood. I wasn't *D*eaf but *d*eaf, and when she signed the lower-case *d* I could almost smell its rotten tang. I'd gone there thinking I'd be embraced like a prodigal daughter and instead found myself under fire for, so I thought—the same curse that had befallen me at the Lions Camp for Crippled Children—not being disabled enough. Hostility makes me hostile in return. It was all I could do not to stick out my tongue and grimace and posture like a Maori warrior. I walked out of there thinking they were a closed, provincial bunch and I was better off outside their preachy little circle. I remained smug in my lowercase superiority until a few years later when I developed a crush on a deaf woman who was a consultant for the PBS television series for disabled children I was cowriting. She spoke as well as signed and it was she who told me these stories.

Once upon a time in certain institutions for the deaf, Sign was out of fashion and something called total communication was in. Total communication simply meant that deaf children would be taught any and all ways to communicate, and that meant lip reading as well as Sign. In some places the message got skewed and in those places the fashion of the day became for deaf children, all deaf children, to learn to lip-read and speak. Sign was frowned upon if not strictly forbidden. As an expert lip-reader I can tell you, lip-reading is a true talent and hard as hell to learn. Most people never can.

The children who couldn't learn to lip-read tried to please their teachers by moving their lips while mimicking what they thought were the right sounds. But the sounds they made were random, based on raw physicality, the feel of air moving through the throat and head. Hearing parents didn't like their children vocalizing this way, because it was too close, they complained to the teachers, to the grunting of animals. If the sounds the children were making weren't the "perfect" ones, their teachers would tape the children's mouths as punishment. The children were trying their hardest to please, to communicate, so they'd gesture as they tried to form the shapes of the words in their minds, shapes for which they had no sounds. That struck their teachers and their parents again as looking too animal, too vulgar, too much like Sign, so to teach them better, the teachers would tie the children's hands to their chairs. "Read the lips," they were told over and over again, but those children couldn't do more than guess what they were being asked to read. It was next to impossible for them to find the essence of elusive sounds in the swift motion of the mouth. Many of them grew up without language—a whole generation who couldn't speak, couldn't sign, and could barely read or write.

She had other stories to tell me too, of unbearable disregard. A child was born to hearing parents, both doctors, full of high expectation for their children, but this infant girl wasn't thriving like her two brothers. She seemed indifferent to language, slow to respond to the simplest commands. They were ambitious, busy people who had no time to waste on a child who was, for whatever reason, less than perfect. They diagnosed her themselves as being mentally retarded and had her committed as a toddler to a state institution. Years later a new attendant who was fond of the child noticed her collecting gum from under the tables and chairs. As he watched her fashion intricate and fantastical figures from the raw material, it began to dawn on him that a mistake had been made. He stood behind her and clapped his hands. She didn't respond. That was all it took to find out she was simply deaf.

Years later I met that girl. By then she had become an artist, living on her own. She wore two hearing aids like mine and also had pulled off a miracle—she not only signed, she lip-read. She vocalized too. But when we talked, I remember thinking how interesting it was that her facial expressions were identical to those of the brother and sister I knew from special ed. I never shared my observation with her. I didn't want her to be disturbed about something she couldn't change. Besides, she probably already knew the oddities of her own speech, the same way I know that when I talk—despite all my pains—the words out of my mouth are cottony, blurry around the edges, as if they're in danger of being swallowed back down my throat. Exactly the way a little-*d* deaf like me *would* speak.

On Being Told No

ONE SIDE EFFECT of my deafness is that I'm always presuming a physical intimacy, usually where there is none. It can get me into trouble and often has. I can't tell you the number of ill-conceived affairs I've had as an adult that started with me putting my hand on someone's collarbone (which conducts sound like a hollow reed) and fastening my gaze on their lips as if it were all I could do not to bite. It was an inadvertent pickup technique I ought to have found (but didn't) shameful and misleading. When I was eleven, though, I was tied into knots over that excessive need of mine to touch and be touched. All my easy sexual play with the boys was turning furtive and guilty even as my romantic awe of the girls was metamorphosing into something sweaty and insistent. I didn't know what my racing heart was telling me about desire, but there was no mistaking the root of my longing—to connect. Hearing is usually the way people connect without touching. Sans that sense I had no way of keeping people at a safe psychic distance while I tussled with my impulse to wrestle them to the ground. My young body felt burdened by itself, by all the things it craved doing but didn't dare, by the inertia of that "special" world it had been thrust into, and by the naked exposure of my secret failings.

Our family life that year was undergoing its own transformations. In 1961 my father retired from the army and got a job driving a cab. As an army family, we'd been used to a certain degree of privilege. The army bases where we lived were mini worlds with their own doctors, housing, schools, and stores, called post exchanges, where military personnel could buy cigarettes, toilet paper, milk, and leather coats at a steep discount. You could get a physical, work out in a gym, or have your teeth fixed all courtesy of the United States government. In Germany we even had live-in help, paid to keep the house clean, watch over us all, and fix dinner at night. We felt flush and cared for.

When Daddy mustered out and the props were snatched away, we suddenly realized we'd only been playing at being well-to-do. When we moved from Fort Hood to Austin, it was to a modest house on the south side, then one of the poorer parts of the city. My sister Trudy, by then seventeen, had changed her name to Gail (a change she'd been planning since her very first day of ballet in postwar Stuttgart, when the German dance instructor pronounced her name Truddy, as in Cruddy). As Gail she ditched her glasses for contacts and enrolled in the theater department at the University of Texas. She'd won a partial scholarship and worked odd jobs but lacked cash for books and tuition. There just wasn't enough money to make ends meet, so Mother went to work at the Big Bear food store as a meat wrapper. We still had a maid, this one a lean, dark woman who, like my mother, resented having to work and slapped her iron against our shirts and blouses as if she were punching someone in the solar plexus. Tenley and I were wary of her. We knew there was no love in her for us. She'd look at us with cold, accusing eyes as if we were the reason she couldn't be with her own two children, exactly our age, who were at home by themselves while she folded our clothes and fixed us dinner.

That year everyone in our house was busy dealing with their own upheavals, even dreamy little Tenley, who faced the cold awakening of first grade. If I were going to make my life a happy one I'd have to do it on my own. That may be why at age eleven I made the calculated decision to quit acting pissed off at my glasses and hearing aids and use them instead as comic props. Laurel and Hardy, Buster Keaton, Charlie Chaplin, Red Skelton, the Three Stooges, Lucille Ball, Carol Burnett, Jerry Lewis, and Daffy Duck: that was the comic cluster of gods at whose feet I worshipped, so I'd learned all the good tricks. With their movie and TV guidance I started cultivating a talent for risk and self-mockery that turned me into my own early version of *Jackass*. I'd open the classroom door with a too-quick jerk and whack myself on the nose so hard it would send my glasses flying. I'd aim for the wadded-up napkin on the cafeteria floor and pratfall right on my butt. I'd flatten my body against the school staircase and bump down the filthy steps like a steamrolled cartoon cat. I'd run full tilt toward the outside cinderblock wall of the gym and scrabble up it until gravity lost me and I'd drop. My no-holds-barred clowning made my deafness just another part of the joke, and when I'd jolt or thump or wallop or bang, I made sure my hearing aids would ring like mini sirens so I could scream, "I'm a bomb!" and explode in a shower of spit. I even embraced the despised slurring blur of my speech after I inadvertently discovered, when my English class took turns reading Truman Capote's *A Christmas Memory* aloud, that a lisp could be used to great comic effect. By the time I was twelve I had cemented my reputation as a class clown with a temper and a streak of the wild. It would take me another two years before I'd slow down on the tricks enough to reawaken to my own body and realize I could use all that excess of feeling as a different way to hear.

I owe that discovery to a tendresse I developed at age fourteen for Suzanne Wood Brown, my high school speech and debate teacher, just out of college and still something of a teenager herself. She was a tall, big-boned woman with a bit of an overbite. She had shrewd brown eyes and nice thick lips that always seemed to be mildly smiling. In the fashion of the time she wore her light brown hair in a high-rise beehive.

At my hypersensitive age, little things pushed me into furious crushes. Teachers who remembered to spell my first name with a *y* could expect every blessed holiday commemorated by Mardi Gras beads, plastic loving cups, chocolate roses, or minty little hearts stamped with my sentiments exactly. The lack-loves who spelled my name with an *i* could expect an in-class vintage performance of deaf incomprehension the likes of which only the brothers Mike and Nicky had seen. After my string of "Huh? What? Could you repeat that again? I'm sorry, I don't understand," had sent the offending teacher into chagrined retreat, I would snicker under my breath, "Terri—the devil's poodle."

My crush on Suzanne went way beyond the correct use

of *y*. She was one of the few teachers not taken aback when I zeroed in on her. Once when I came barreling into her classroom, glasses askew and hearing aids abuzz, she raised her eyebrows and commanded me to sit, as if I were a skittering puppy. She leaned over, pushed my ear molds back into place, settled my glasses back on my face, then gave my forehead a leisurely little flick with her finger. From that gesture on I was hers. Suzanne didn't flinch from the energy and desperation of my devotion. She simply used it the same way Dolores, my Bambi love, had at Lions Camp—to get me to do what she wanted. What Suzanne wanted was for me to learn to speak clearly, without a lisp, without a slur, so that what I said wouldn't be obscured by the way I said it. I don't know why she loved me as much as she did. Other teachers gave me their time and attention, but hers was so particular, so physical. I once told her, when I put my hand on her back as she was talking, that it felt as if the words were vibrating in my palm as she said them.

Thereafter, when my voice slipped into a flat, monotonous drone, she'd tease me, trying to coax me out of my habit of thinking how I ought to be hearing so I could concentrate on how the sound was actually moving through skin and bone. She meant to help me find the root physicality of hearing. She'd rest her chin on the back of my head and recite lines from "The Congo," with all those *boomlay BOOM*'s. She wanted me to feel the chanting beat of that Vachel Lindsay poem right inside my skull. She'd press her fingers against my windpipe just hard enough for me to feel the pressure of my own breath as speech in its rawest state. Then she'd put her palms on my cheeks or mold my lips into a little moue, to start me playing with the shapes of my teeth and tongue, so I could use them to refine the crude expulsions of air.

Over the next three years she worked with me like that, using my ardent desire to please her to teach me control over my speech. I would never lose my touch of deaf-speak, that dead giveaway of a lateral lisp. Even now if I let down my guard the words out of my mouth turn gluey and thick. But by age sixteen, after two and a half hard years of effort, I had embraced the pleasure of that discipline so intimately I seldom let down my guard.

I was keeping tight rein over one or two other impulses as well. My visions, contrary to the doctor's long-ago predictions, would still periodically lift me up and away, but the month I turned sixteen I put a stop to that. I'd been cast in the old theatrical warhorse of Thornton Wilder's *Our Town*. I'd never been cast as the ingénue before, always as the comic relief, but I'd worked hard with Suzanne to get my speech cleared up, to get a grip on the slur, to mimic the correct inflections of sentences I couldn't hear. Being cast as pretty, doomed Emily was my reward. On the first night of performance I'd just set foot onstage and before I could get a word out of my mouth I was pulled up into the air and held dangling above the scene. The cafeteria stage, the school, my whole little world—it was like the top of things had blown off once more.

When I saw my body in miniature mouthing words on that tiny stage beneath me, my thought was almost a gripe: *Who in the hell is that saying my lines?* I felt cheated of the whole experience of finally acting the role of a girl, the easiest and hardest role I'd played to date. I'd been dumbstruck to discover the role of ingénue was all about keeping still. Absolutely no energy required. No need to contort my face into a perpetual grimace the way I did when I played that disapproving old starch, Lady Bracknell, or make my jaw go as slack as it could get without drooling when I played the pesky idiot brother in *Antic Spring*. All I had to do was quell my inner cyclone, keep my face immobile, my eyes wide, and my voice loud and precise enough to hear. Then die off quick. During a rehearsal, after my character Emily kicked off and took her place in the town graveyard, one of my male costars blurted out admiringly, "You look great dead!" Since I wasn't in motion, the boys had a chance to look me over, see I actually was a girl and becoming a pretty one at that. It seemed to have shocked them into erections. I couldn't wait to test the effect on a wider audience.

Up aloft in the air on opening night, I felt so damn angry to be missing my anticipated moment of seductive triumph. My next thought was a declaration: *I will never do this again.* The minute I had that thought, the diffused and floating fabric of my being seemed to regather, narrow into a funnel, and pour back into my body. I hadn't missed a single cue, but from that moment on I never again had another vision, never again left my body behind. Although sometimes, even now, looking out my bedroom window at a pumpkin moon or at a thin cold sliver of one, I can feel a pull, almost like a call.

My queer impulse was the other thing I was trying to get under control. I think I must have suspected I was queer from age five, and was happy to discover its sexual component at age seven with a blonde my age named Sunny during a game we called—and to this day I'm embarrassed to remember—"milking the cow." You can well imagine. Around age thirteen I was finally able to put a name to my inner roilings when I looked up the word "homosexuality" in a dictionary. I had heard my older sister use the word with some vehemence when describing to my parents how she'd stumbled upon her female college roommate in bed with a woman, and the fact that I found the context intriguing made me suspect the word had particular relevance to me. The definition in the dictionary, "sexual desire directed at a person of one's own sex," thrilled me to death. But I wanted further clarification. I thought I was being immensely discreet when I offhandedly mentioned at dinner that night that I'd looked up "homosex—." I didn't even have time to finish the word. It was like I'd shot off a gun and stampeded cattle. The commotion it caused left me with the strong impression that homosexual was the wrong side of the sheets to be on.

The dictionary mentioned desire and that's how I imagined homosexual—as being in the throes of longing. I knew longing. It seemed a pretty OK state to be in. Longing had moved me to work hard for all my teachers, but especially the women, because they were gentle with me and that gentleness, besides making me less afraid of disappointing them, made me yearn to please them. That yearning only intensified with Suzanne, who reintroduced me to the pleasures of my own senses. She was passionate with me, passionate about what she saw as my talents. She took chance after chance on me by entering me into dozens of speech competitions. When I finally won one, won a big one, a statewide competition in the reading of poetry, she and her husband at the time took me out for lobster, and she gave me my first sip of champagne right out of her own glass.

It's no wonder I longed for her, that my longing blossomed into an ache I feared, exulted in, and kept in check. Or tried to. The same way I tried to keep my sexual feelings for the boys in check. I liked exploring their bodies, liked the rank smell of them when they'd get excited, liked ducking into the abandoned school alleyways in the early evening to take a peek at a penis in exchange for a squeeze of my breast. And when the oldest of the Reynolds brothers cornered me outside the gym and pushed his pelvis hard into my butt and held me tight like that until he broke into a sweat, I'd liked it. But even though I made endless lists of names for the ten children I thought I might one day have, during those years when abortion was a crime and contraception itself exuded a sulfurous whiff, there was no one more afraid of pregnancy than I, the deaf queer already so taken aback by her own body. I'd touch and let the feeling be mutual, but I wasn't going to get carried away. Not by sex. Not even, if I could help it, by yearning.

I was going to do something with my life. Exactly what, I didn't yet know, but I was almost sure of it. Suzanne had convinced me I was a smart girl, smarter than the nature of my deafness allowed people to see. I'd simply have to work that much harder to let it be known. All my hard work *had* to culminate in something extraordinary. That's what I kept telling myself and what the little horoscope booklet I'd bought, detailing the secret power of Scorpios, was telling me, too. My last year of high school, when we seniors were being called in to consult with the guidance counselor about our paths in life, I couldn't wait to hear what he had to say, what guidance he was going to give me, what great path he was going to suggest. He'd already provided my close friends with brochures from the colleges Suzanne and my sister Gail said were the best—Yale,

Harvard, Princeton, Columbia. When it was my turn to be advised, I was electric with joy. My meeting with him lasted all of five minutes. He glanced up when I opened the door and said, "Oh, you're the one." Then he handed me a brochure that read, errors and all, "Factory work make good job for Deaf."

Passing Strange

WHEN I FELL IN FIRST TRUE LOVE with Dolores at Lions Camp, I became her champion even though she was older than I. I wasn't quite ten. She was *eleven*. She was as sweet as she was beautiful. I knew that if that had been me in that wheeled bed, I wouldn't have been sweet. I'd have been like the floater who spat and hissed like a snake when she was angry. I'd watch that girl pitch her fits, and fill with admiration. She was scary as hell.

My Dolores had the thick-lashed gaze of a gazelle. She liked for me to help get her ready for breakfast in the morning, because it could be embarrassing—you had to empty things—but we'd read *Mad* magazine together so who gave a damn. She knew I was in love with her and used that knowledge to bully me into doing anything she wanted. What she most wanted was for me to push her wheeled bed down all the forbidden hills. We thought that was so illicit, but now I realize they were just bumps in the road, nothing as daunting as we believed. Sometimes I'd push her wheeled bed to the river, or was it just a little creek? We both thought of it as the Rio Grande, and when I moved her head tenderly to the side, we imagined we were looking across to the Mexico of her dreams.

She talked of traveling the world. Maybe she'd teach or be a lawyer. Once she'd entertained the notion of becoming a pediatrician. She loved babies, but she didn't see how she'd be able to take a pulse. She figured that whatever she did, it would have to be something primarily of the mind. She was smart. She was a reader. In the throes of love I said, "You'll be anything in the world you want." But even then I wondered how.

Seven years later, I was asking the same question of myself and had no answer. Walking out of the counselor's office, I'd felt the same terrible loss of heart I'd felt at the Lions Camp right before I decided to drown. I couldn't bring myself to tell Suzanne or my family about my humiliation, but I stopped talking about all the fancy colleges I wanted to attend (Bennington being first on my list because of all the girls). I felt again as if some calculating presence had been looking over my shoulder all this time, judging my chances for a happy life and concluding (as I always did) that I had none. I don't know why I gave in so easily. Maybe because love seemed to have failed me. The guidance counselor didn't know me, couldn't love me the way my family or even Suzanne did. I realized then that love alone wouldn't be enough to save me from the weight of what seemed a whole other world of disregard. Without the protections of love, the only weapon I had in the arsenal of my own defense was accomplishment. And the only real evidence I had of my high school accomplishments was the partial scholarship I'd won to the University of Texas in Austin.

College wasn't a given in our family. In Europe we'd been part of a conquering elite, the American military abroad, but our German maids had been better educated than either of my parents. My mother had dropped out of high school. My dad, although a genius in languages, had just a high school degree. Yet we still considered ourselves standard-bearers for the superiority of our country, its intellectual power and moral claim. We had something of the same hauteur when we lived in the small Texas town of Killeen, which was dominated by the Fort Hood army base. But when Daddy took early retirement and we all moved to Austin, we were just civilians again and fell back into our actual class. If college wasn't a given in our family, hard work was. After my father retired from the military at age forty-eight, he spent two years driving a cab by day, then staying up half the night attending classes and hitting the books so he could finally get his college degree in social work. Gail had worked just as hard at her studies, taking her term papers with her to her job as a night attendant in the state institution for the insane. Until we left the military, my mother had never had to work a day in her life, but in Austin, with money scarce, she got that job as a meat wrapper at Big Bear, and then one she hated a little less, as a floor saleswoman at Parisian Peyton's fine fashions for women. Little Tenley was all of ten and a half when she started babysitting the Brettschott's adopted infant boy, and she hasn't stopped working at some hard job or other since.

By the time I was ready to graduate high school, I'd never held any kind of job, not even babysitting. I was never expected to work, and I'd never questioned that expectation. I'd always just assumed my family agreed with Granny Doris that God had something special planned for me. But after the guidance counselor shut his door on me,

I began to fear that maybe my family was as doubtful about my future as I'd been of my first true love's. When I told my mother what the counselor had said, showed her the brochure I'd crumpled up and pushed to the bottom of my purse, I went cold when I saw her smooth it out and read it over carefully, consideringly.

A few years ago in an upstairs closet of my parents' ranchetta in Texas, I found the box of letters my sister Gail had written to me during that time. She had by then moved to New York and married. I'd sent her sheaves of weeping, sardonic letters ranting about my fate, telling her everything that I wanted to spare my parents. Factory work. Was that all my smarts were good for? All my struggle to get the words out right, to bring another kind of meaning to my life. And what about what Suzanne called my exceptional talent in performance? Was that promise just another lie? If it was, it was a lie I couldn't help but embrace, and what kind of a loser is that desperate for self-belief? All her letters of reply kept saying, "You can do this. The counselor is an idiot. The world is wrong." Gail reminded me repeatedly that I had won a scholarship to study theater at the University of Texas just like she had. If she could do it, why couldn't I?

When we were five and twelve years old in Berlin, Trudy/Gail and I had been guinea pigs for one of our daddy's extracurricular spy experiments in parasensory perception. We were put in separate rooms, where we took turns projecting mental images of triangles, stars, crosses, or circles on the flash cards we were shown at timed intervals. A high score was 5 out of 25. We scored 20 out of the 25, not just once but every single time they tested us (all of twice). Even from afar, my big sister held sway.

But the capper came when my brother-in-law Tim scrawled his bold-point PS at the end of one of Gail's missives. Tenley and I had fallen hard for Tim the day he drove up in his red MG to take our sister to a Killeen High School sock hop. A military brat and a commander's son, he wore khakis and button-down shirts in a culture composed of local cowboys in jeans and T-shirts with cigarette packs rolled up in the sleeves. Dark-haired and slender, with a comically mobile face and a wide, amused grin, Tim was a cute man who remained cute even after he grew the beard that made him look professorially distinguished. He became the object of our instant and intense adoration, not only because he so obviously delighted in our big sister but because his killer imitations of Mick Jagger in full scream or Roddy McDowall *ooh eeeking* in *Planet of the Apes* gave our mother the giggles. During the early years of Gail and Tim's marriage, Tenley and I would follow him from room to room pretending to be a pack of bloodhounds, *arrooohing* in his wake until Gail would finally tell us to knock it off and grow up. As I grew older, my dog-like devotion to him remained every bit as intense, if more subtle. If Tim professed an interest in Native American pottery, I would make endless drawings of the same; if he liked a bicycle called the Bob Jackson, I, too, would profess myself an ardent fan. Even now, years after Tim put his pipes aside, I sometimes light up my slender rosewood churchwarden with its rhinestone collar, just to wreath myself in the aroma of his tobacco. Tenley and I had dubbed him Timbo-God and worshipped accordingly. So when he added his two cents to Gail's, telling me I needed to heed my big sister, it was as if Zeus had seconded Hera.

When I was seventeen, fortified by that advice from

on high, I marched right up the steps to the University of Texas Drama Department, scholarship in hand, and asked to be advised. The adviser took a long look at my hearing aids, then said, "You're deaf," as if I didn't already know it. His next word was, "Costuming." I was puzzled. I don't know how to dress, never have, still look mismatched and ill-fitted. As for sewing, in high school home economics I'd been ostracized for stitching my thumb to the hem of someone else's skirt. The costume shop loomed cold as Siberia. I told him as much. He didn't once smile. It was the costume shop or nothing. They wouldn't allow me on that stage. Not to act. Not to direct. Not in that department. Then he said again, as if it were the whole explanation, "You're deaf."

I hate being told no, but the word in itself never had the power to crush me. What always did me in was the stare that accompanied the no. The stare is a look that, even as it presumes to know all about you, really just intends to put you in your place, to remind you of your unworthiness relative to the one who is looking upon you. The stare tells you that you are not *it*; you are not in the least what the beholder wishes to behold. You either do not engage its interest enough to count or you have somehow managed to offend its eye. This man advising me felt privileged by his presumed intellect, his supposed talent, his obvious physical beauty, and by the authority of his job, to proscribe worth. And in his eyes I didn't have any. With his stare in full bore, I couldn't even begin to argue with him. I was a good enough actor to get myself out of that office, smiling, even nodding as if I agreed. Inside I crackled with fury both at him and at myself for my shuffling, grinning exit.

But I was again making up my mind. I'd show him. Even if I didn't yet know how.

I was growing up pre–Americans with Disabilities Act, when there was nothing in the way of accommodation for big-*D* or little-*d* deaf, or any other of the disabled for that matter. Schools provided no translators or note takers for disabled kids who were mainstreamed. We were left to fend for ourselves, learn as best we could. There were no captions for the deaf at the movies or on TV, which may be why I grew up favoring action flicks and foreign films. Computers were still huge monsters housed in warehouses, and text messaging was done by telegraph. In college, when I needed to get up in time for class or an appointment, there were no flashing or vibrating clocks to alert me. I'd have to impose on someone to wake me up in the morning or do what I usually did and try to trick my body into waking when it should.

I was a private, fiercely independent kid who had liked fending for herself. It killed me, when I was living in an off-campus dorm, to know that five o'clock could be a lonely time for my mother at home and that I couldn't just pick up the phone and call her, let her know I was OK and loved her. These days I can do just that—pick up a cell phone and text message. Or if I need to speak directly with someone, I can pick up a phone, put the receiver on a little machine called a TTY that looks like a typewriter, punch in 711, and an operator, with whom I am connected by text messaging, will place my phone calls for me. Before TTYs and text messaging, if I wanted to do something as simple as call in an order for pizza, I had to collar someone, friend or kind stranger, who didn't mind translating the scintillating details of pepperoni versus sausage and would keep their own opinions (*sausage!*) to themselves. I felt envious watching my friends casually chatting on phones with their families, their lovers, their friends—ordering takeout, reserving a car or a restaurant, booking a ticket on a plane or to a play, summoning 911, making a prank call, a dental appointment, a movie date. Conducting the business of their everyday lives all by themselves, the way every adult should be able to do.

My deafness had the power to infantilize me then. And make me fearful. One late night I was walking back to my rented room with an armful of books from the library. When I got to the front door, I dropped my key and bent down to pick it up. When I straightened back up there was a man looming behind me. I managed a squeak, which was meant to be the word "help," threw my armload of books at him, and thrust my key in front of me like a dagger. He hadn't intended to scare me, hadn't come to rape and kill me, was there to meet his girlfriend for a date. But I hadn't heard him coming up behind me, even though he wasn't trying to be sneaky or even particularly quiet. That little heart thumper, just like Scare, reminded me of everything that *could* happen because it *does* happen. And if it did happen my deafness could, as I'd just been reminded, leave me as oblivious to threat as any bikinied bimbo in a B-movie horror flick. Being rendered both clueless and frightened made me furious. Neither fear nor bimbo-ness were the ways of a male, and even though no one could tell by the way I looked or dressed—I was by then a long-haired, pretty girl who wore tailored A-line dresses and heels—my secret self was still a laughing, unflappable, intrepid boy.

I had long since traded my box hearing aids for two behind-the-ear numbers easily hidden by the curtain of my long, dark hair. But if a classmate or a teacher noticed and remarked on them, I found it easy to smile and claim to be only slightly hard of hearing. I developed an almost maniacal intensity in class (often mistaken for rapt attention) because I knew that if I relaxed my attention even the slightest bit I wouldn't understand a word anybody was saying. I took on a disdainful air at parties, hoping that no one would ask me something I couldn't instantly reply to; and if anyone struck up a conversation, I'd monologue, a long, one-sided yak, so I wouldn't slip up and reveal what I was or wasn't really hearing. I wasn't going to let anyone call me a "deaf woman," a label I was sure made me sound dumb and cow-like, enveloped in a protective silence that denied me my complexity. Passing as hearing took such a toll that passing as straight was a piece of cake.

In high school I'd loved being physical with boys, but I'd kept my legs crossed tight when it came down to actual intercourse. It used to make me sick to my stomach when rumors would swirl about the girls who missed a period or two and then would suddenly "disappear" from class. The rumors were usually spread by the boys who had knocked them up. I liked boys, but I didn't trust them much. I suspected they were just as scummy and self-serving as I was when it came to their own desires.

I hated the idea of having to take responsibility for the sex. I didn't want to have to bother with a diaphragm or a spermicide or a coil or birth control pills. It rankled me that all the boys had to do was whip it out and, maybe, if they felt like it, cover it with latex. I thought, *To hell with that.* But my resentment didn't do much to soothe my lust, which may be why I became such a tease. I just couldn't resist having mock sex with men I liked, like the cute blond TA in the English Department whom I thought of as being old at twenty-four. I'd go to his office to be advised and we'd end up on his desk, him fingering me through my panties or me naked sitting on him, fully clothed. It was thrilling and had not one whit to do with love.

I was still mooning over the girls I had crushes on, wondering how the hell I could ever have sex with one. That was a real worry: how to have sex with another woman—not just getting a woman to want to have sex with me but, once that piece of the puzzle was in place, how to literally get it done. I had no real physical experience with other girls, except that long-ago grope with the little girl my age, Sunny. I used to kiss the color photo of Julie Christie I'd ripped out of *Life* magazine and force myself to imagine something going on down there, but I couldn't wrap my mind around it. Vaginas seemed too complicated. Sex with men, especially mock sex, was (for me at least) a lot easier, a lot less confusing. I wasn't invested in outcomes, so sex with men was something over which I had control. And I was cultivating control.

No one was going to know I was deaf. No one was going to know I was queer and wanting. No one was going to know that inside my smiling pretty-girl exterior I was so frustrated, fearful, and mad it was making me mean as a snake. I went through men like tissues, kept my hearing aids hidden, got contacts, wore hard little heels and prim little jumpers, and took laxatives and practiced self-induced vomiting to keep myself in fighting trim. Control. Getting control. But my throat was rubbed raw and my hearing aids buzzed and I didn't know it, and my hair wouldn't stay in place, and nothing would stay ironed. And sometimes as I lay talking with the girl from Waco, who charmed me with her overenunciation, on one of the beds in the small room we rented together at the edge of campus, it was all I could do not to reach out and run my finger around the curve of her naked ear.

I was bound to come undone. It happened the first month of my sophomore year. I sat down to take a biology exam and began to cry, and not just because it was my worst subject. I wasn't sobbing or anything like that, it was just tears pouring down my face. I put the test aside, stood up, and walked out of the classroom. I spent the next three days in the university clinic, crying like a baby. My mother came to visit me my first day there, but she was at a loss. I'd never shown her this part of me before, this kind of giving in. I knew from the uncertainty in her eyes that she had no idea how to help me through this. After she left, I sat up in that bed and let my tears evaporate. It was time to face a few things. I couldn't meet everything head-on all at once, especially not my scarily pent-up sexuality—that would take more years of clandestine experimentation. But I could make a start.

When I started telling people I was really deaf, I did it with a grim determination that was almost funny. Some people reacted exactly the way I feared; they'd shy away, get self-conscious or rude, and cut our conversations short as if they'd suddenly been told they were talking into a void. There were others who assumed I was an unsullied innocent, and who would inquire in carefully enunciated sentences, "Dooo youuuu drink liq-uoooor?" But it surprised me how many people were just plain sweet. They wanted to know the best way to be understood, took pains to talk directly to my face, and didn't insult me by using words of one syllable. It was in part that gentle acceptance that made me more curious about my own deafness.

Always, before, it had been an affliction to wrestle as one would wrestle angels. But after I finally accepted it as an inevitable part of my life, I felt free to do a little exploring. I've always been able to hear with hearing aids—that is, I could discern noise as a distant roaring in my consciousness, and when there were many people talking together, I'd hear them as a strange music, like the hum of some intricate machine. As unclear and peculiar as they might be, the humming and the roaring still made a kind of sense to me. It was silence that I was afraid to face. I started my first fearful explorations of it tentatively, taking off my hearing aids during the day and then going through an hour, an afternoon, as long as I could take it, in the same absolute quiet of my nights.

It felt like a secret vice to enter a world stripped of sound. The silence there wasn't empty, just full of its own secrets. I could lie on my mattress with my eyes closed and know someone was coming into the apartment, because the hardwood floor would shudder and that would set the metal wheels and frame of my bed to quivering. When I'd give a date a hug or a kiss, I'd feel the body trembling its real welcome, the sex smell rising from the flesh like heat off asphalt. Life became instantly more immediate when nothing was going on in the world but what was right in front of me, what I could see, taste, touch, and smell, what the prickling of my skin could tell me. And yes, that's a danger, but it's also a thrill. The only trouble was, I kept lusting after sound.

Drag Acts

MY MOTHER, EDNA, likes to tell stories about the Free Holiness church she went to as a child in Dads Corner, Texas. Everyone in her family loved to sing, and the way she tells it they were always going to the church to perform or to see others perform. The people in her church didn't like their religion too organized—they wanted a place where anyone could walk in off the streets and worship—so the preachers were usually itinerant ones who could be sent on their way if they proved too sour or dull. The traveling evangelistic groups she described who came to those oil-patch towns to preach seemed like one of the traveling theater troupes of old—loud, colorful, full of eye-catching tricks. They were the only real entertainment those small towns had, and they were always bringing in new wonders, like the singing duo of white-skinned, raven-haired little girls dressed head to toe in black velvet, who sang more lustily than the honky-tonkers in the bar down the street.

When the congregation prayed for someone who was hurting, that was a performance as well, starting with the public confessions of sin. "Lord forgive me," one young mother wailed and wept, "I made my little Darlene stand at the window to keep an eye out for her daddy while I was fornicating with the neighbor." "Fornication" was a word my five-year-old mother heard said quite a lot. The minister and members of the congregation would anoint the head of the suffering with oil and then everyone would put their hands on that poor soul to pray the devil out. Someone in the group might suddenly start speaking in a different tongue and then things would get real quiet. Everyone would listen hard, because nobody could understand what was being said and it might be something important, a coded message from heaven or hell. Then after five minutes or so the gibberish would suddenly start to make sense to some listener and they'd start translating the message for the rest. Usually the message was about saving your soul, or everyone having to be ready 'cause the end was nigh, or a mark-of-the-Beast prediction straight out of Revelations.

Evening services could last until midnight, and when the praying and speaking in tongues would finally stop, her daddy would invite the whole crowd over to the Cunningham house, where her mother would cook up hotcakes, coffee, and ham for the multitudes. After everyone had eaten their fill, they'd start telling stories or singing. When they sang, it was the kind of music still strange then to church: boisterous, almost rowdy, with a twanging poignancy like a spark of new life coming. Those nights, the whole congregation stayed up until three or four in the morning, singing all the holy songs you could think of. My mother says that kind of worship was like the conjuring of joy and took the place of psychiatry and really did change lives. Add sex, liquor, and drugs to that mix and you've got the flavor of my life in theater.

Some people think it odd that I'm as passionate as I am about theater. They point out to me, as people are often wont to do, that I'm deaf. The very word suggests it's harder for me to do everything that spoken theater requires—get my cues, enunciate tongue-twisting phrases, project enough to reach the back of an auditorium, give sentences nuanced (or even any) inflection. And it is true that those things, which come so naturally to the hearing body, aren't natural to me at all, especially clear speech, which requires the same passionate hyperattention as lip reading. But Suzanne had taught me well. With her training and my persistence, the acts of speech, like lip reading, became subsumed into a semiconscious state of alert I'm not even aware of until those odd moments when my jaw starts aching. Then I'll realize I've been forcing my tongue down and pushing my teeth up so my *s*'s won't hiss quite so much.

I sometimes imagine a split in time and being, where one of me goes on to learn Sign and ends up starring (as I know I would) in National Theatre of the Deaf. But theater for the deaf didn't exist when I was a kid. It came later, after I was grown and already so in love with speech, I didn't want to give it up. I was enthralled by the effects spoken words could have, like another kind of music. If you said a word like "you" in a deep-enough whisper, as a single, powerful syllable, it became a rumbling growl, almost accusing, that meant, "Come to me." And saying it that way could actually make someone come to you like a spell of enchantment. I was even in love with the effort it took me to speak precisely, meaningfully. There's a pride in it, the same I've seen in a ballerina or an off-duty Marine walking down a street, their discipline in their shoulders, in the plant of their feet.

I knew even as I worked at it that my speech would never be perfect, that I'd always need help, always need someone who wouldn't be afraid to tell me if I was mispronouncing a word or speaking too softly or with too much of a slur to be understood. So I knew too that there was truth in that theater adviser's rejection of me when I had gone to him full of hope, my scholarship in hand. He'd been right to tell me no. Where he came from, theater wasn't simply an art, it was a business. And while art can delight in the unruly if it's passionate enough, business demands a moneymaking perfect. There were so many perfect people out in the world wanting to do the same things I wanted to do, he knew I'd never be able to make it on a professional stage, not the way "professional" was then defined. I knew it, too. If I was going to make my own life a happy one, if I was going to remain the hero of my own story, fulfilling my own quests, I knew I'd have to find some netherworld of theater where people were less interested in what I couldn't do than in what I could, where the action onstage was just as important as the words compelling it. And I found them. Found the people and found the places, even if sometimes I had to create those places for myself.

You had to be actively looking for these odd places, because they were funky, out-of-the-way warehouses, barns, garages, salsa bars, cafes, places you wouldn't typically expect to harbor art. Usually they had some kind of a makeshift stage, or even just an empty space marked out on the floor. There were always cushions, folding chairs, benches, or an assortment of household-furniture castaways for people watching to sit on. Even the poorest of these theaters had lights for their stages, if only a couple of tin funnels with 60-watt bulbs.

I had imagined the theater world as a cold, body-obsessed, hierarchical, and hostile place since the day that department adviser had turned me away. But in these found Shangri-las of art and neglect where everyone smoked dope, drank a bit, and seemed more in pursuit of play than perfection, deafness didn't seem to matter. I could fall flat on my butt, be crappy, and who cared? Those were the places where failure was just a part of trying. But usually I didn't fail, because all the things that could nudge me into a meltdown—the crippling self-consciousness and almost automatic self-loathing that can come with feeling imperfect—weren't there. What was present in abundance was a reckless joy, the sense that even if what you were doing was dead serious, it was being done in a spirit of play. The audiences in those places weren't just a block of ticket holders who had paid to be entertained; they were either actually or potentially our friends, and they'd come for the late-night camaraderie as much as for the show. They'd spit or boo just as enthusiastically as they'd cheer, and they didn't hesitate to give us their own personal on-the-spot reviews. It was with those kinds of audiences, in those small, sometimes seedy playhouses, that I was actually able to experience, not just read about, acts of epiphany so intense that my love of theater became and remains one of religious devotion. It may or may not be coincidental that I experienced almost all of them when I was dressed as a man.

The first of these queer little epiphanies happened when I was nineteen years old during a performance of Shakespeare in a Texas town so tiny it wasn't even on the state map. Shakespeare at Winedale originated as a University of Texas summer English class taught by James B. Ayres, a long-legged, barrel-chested man with a broad, shrewd, handsome face who had once been a minor-league baseball player, until his jaw was shattered by a line drive. With Ayres, Shakespeare is a high-energy undertaking, a team sport, with the audience as involved in the performances as they'd be in a championship game. He handpicked the squad of us who would be living together for six weeks in that lonely patch of east-central hill country, studying the plays of Shakespeare by performing them, in an old hay barn that resembled an Elizabethan theater.

Winedale itself is a German farming community with a combined population, then, of about twenty. One hot August afternoon we were rehearsing the tavern scene from *Henry IV,* part 1, with a keg of beer. Our set was just a couple of picnic tables we'd plunked down in the middle of the dirt floor of the barn.

I had learned to compensate for the still-uneven clarity of my speech by honing a raw physical talent for playing comic roles, especially those that called for the body to risk itself in play. I'd do what other performers wouldn't—fall knocked-cold in the mud, slither on my back down a flight of stairs, charge full tilt screaming through the audience waving a sword in my hand. Ayres liked his Shakespeare at breakneck speed with a sense of high risk and scary improvisation. Fearlessness counted for almost as much as the clarity of the words being spoken. He also thought it good training for women to play male roles, not just because the whole history of Shakespeare is a gender-bending one, but because cross-casting was a new way to study the text. All of which is why I was decked out that afternoon, with a glued-on beard and a pillow in my pants, hoisting a pewter mug full of beer, as fat, old, scruffy Sir John Falstaff, looking, my mother told me later when she saw the show, just like my Grandpa Chuck.

Our makeshift tavern was open-air and sweltering and the beer was cold. It went fast and did its duty. Shakespeare didn't feel intimidating anymore but fun and sociable. Maybe it was the beer, but during that rehearsal-as-party all of us in the barn suddenly *got* the performance we were doing, and understood this most famous of tavern scenes, which pits the tubby old crook Falstaff in a battle of wits with Prince Hal, the spoiled heir-designate to the English throne. It's a class war, actually, that comes to a climax in a silly game of mimicry that odd couple are "playing."

Most of us instinctively allied ourselves with Falstaff, laughing at his antics, his playfulness, his language. We liked him. He was a lot more like us than the snotty Prince Perfect. But in this play the prince and Falstaff are friends, so we were willing to give Hal a little leeway.

Then comes the moment when the comedy suddenly dries up and Prince Hal turns mean. He's informed that his father the king is dying and the country is at war. If he wants to inherit the kingdom, it's high time for him to get back to being royal. In his first conscious act as a would-be king, he reveals that he feels himself to be everyone's superior, cutting his ties with us, meaning Falstaff and the rest of the commoner riffraff. But Hal doesn't like looking like the bad guy. So he does what every skilled manipulator does when they want to end a relationship that turns irksome. He sharpens his gaze. He fixes on Falstaff's flaws, not just looking *at* them, but *for* them, with a savage and avid eye. Then he uses his wit to enumerate these many and damning imperfections. Falstaff is no longer Hal's shrewdly amusing confidant and friend but an enemy, a *them*—a distasteful, old, white-bearded Satan.

In the face of such betrayal it is amazing that Falstaff can find the courage to rise up to his own defense, much less to ours. But in this scene that's exactly what he does, of course. Now, this is Shakespeare, and we were just a bunch of kids, but we all understood what was happening—Falstaff put himself like a shield between us and power as embodied by the laconic prince, who really didn't like us much and wouldn't have been in that tavern drinking with us if he hadn't been so amused and intrigued by Falstaff himself. Falstaff's devil-may-care sense of life as play is so enviable, so deeply rebellious, it's kind of a shock to think of it as a defensive tactic. But in that mock-up of a tavern, it becomes startlingly clear that he is playing for his life, and for ours. And when the prince betrays his sly old friend, leaving him behind, publicly rebuked, humiliated, and alone, we were surprised to find ourselves feeling not just sad but anguished. We didn't know then that we'd only caught a glimmer of what that scene would eventually make us feel.

The weekend of our first performance, the audience seemed huge to us. Over three hundred people had driven the sixty miles from Austin or the fifty from Houston or the forty-five from San Antonio to see our class presentation of ten scenes from six plays. They were a wonderful crowd—they too had been drinking beer—and the tavern scene came toward the end of a raucous evening. By the time our scene opened I was hysterical with emotion. I couldn't believe I was there. Me, old mush mouth, performing Shakespeare! And in a role I adored. I was giddy with love for Shakespeare, Falstaff, Ayres, the audience, the other kids at Winedale, even myself. It felt as if we'd all somehow been chosen for what seemed like a miracle—the hilarious, wild air of what we were creating. We were the most imperfect group of performers you could ever imagine, and our audience was suffocating in the heat of that summer night, but we had been transported beyond caring. That small, packed barn in the middle of nowhere might as well have been the center of the world.

I waltzed around the dirt floor of the barn, in the guise of my own secret role of protector, defender, and goof, making the audience love me. I could feel it happen when they did. And I was glad I'd made them love me, the way they ought to love Falstaff. Because I knew then and there that Falstaff and I were going to defeat that snot ball who called himself a prince. That's when I felt myself suddenly fall into the language. I was in the middle of Falstaff's great defense of himself and his kind—the comic relief, the dispossessed, the poor, the ill, the imperfect—those for whom destiny had little say. And the words began to resonate, deep in my body, in the air—what Shakespeare had written, what Falstaff had to say, what was happening in that barn, what I was feeling at that moment.

My friend Jan, a tall, slender boy with a sharp, autocratic face, who was playing Hal, felt the language turn real, as it was meant to, and he kept turning it. The audience felt it, too—the shivering emotion in those words was what they and we had come to experience, although none of us quite realized it until Prince Hal's last two lines as he leaves Falstaff and the habitués of the tavern behind. Falstaff beseeches Hal to remember that if he banishes the old fool Falstaff from his company, he will be banishing all the world. The prince says just four words in reply: "I do. I will." That awful moment of denunciation is one of breathtaking cruelty; and as those two lines were uttered the temperature in the barn dropped ten degrees and every person in it turned stark still. All of us, audience, performers, and whatever ghosts were in the rafters, were caught up together in an enormous swell of shared emotion so complex I can only call it love, in all its woe and wonder.

Among the hundreds of people who were there that night, our shared moment of recognition became a family memory, and even as it was happening I thought, *I'll never be this caught up, this swept away, again, nothing this miraculous will ever happen to me again.* But it did.

After I'd graduated from UT with a degree in American studies, I'd taken a job teaching poetry as part of an afternoon program for at-risk elementary school kids, but the grant had run out and wasn't renewed. The summer of 1976, I was a twenty-five-year-old at very loose ends and found myself wandering around Austin looking for refuge from my poverty and boredom. At the University of Texas I'd taken a television scripting and performance course that seemed to have attracted some of the wilder, more off-beat rejects of the theater program. It was there that I met Shannon, a tall, blond, Germanic-looking woman who, when she puts on her heels and her shiny red dress, recalls Faye Dunaway. Shannon and her boyfriend, Michael, a mild-looking, gray-eyed man with soft, flyaway hair and a manner that belies his sinewy muscularity, had opened up a beer and music joint in Austin called Liberty Lunch. One afternoon as I munched a gratis muffalata, Shannon told me that she and Michael were opening another place down on Sixth Street. Would I like to drop by some night and do one of the weird little skits I used to write for the television performance course?

Midnight of that day I showed up, scripts in hand, at Esther's Pool. Esther's is a former salsa bar/pool hall, with limestone walls, a wooden floor, one small unisex bathroom, and a long, high, wide window that looked out onto the life of Sixth Street, which at the time wasn't jumping. The joint was either christened for gay icon and Technicolor swimming star Esther Williams or for the pool tables left by the last deadbeat tenant. The place had no stage. It did have that scattering of pool tables. And it had a microphone smack-dab in front of the huge, wide window. When I first walked in there, Shannon, dressed in glittering red, was holding onto that mike for dear life, crooning in comic parody of a big-band diva. People were sitting on the floor, lounging at the bar, or waiting for the singing to stop so they could pop the eight ball into the side pocket. Outside, passersby plastered their mugs against the window, putting on their own little shows for those of us inside, sticking out their tongues or shooting the finger or just staring through the glass like snakes mesmerized by a mongoose. I felt perfectly at home.

Sixth Street in Austin nowadays is compared to the old Bourbon Street in New Orleans, one long, partying strip, but in the late '70s it had a forlorn, neglected air. No one ever ventured downtown after five o'clock unless they were looking for a drink, a whore, or a fight. Right next door to Esther's little building was a "massage" parlor, and down the street another bar where the city garbagemen hung out and got into occasional fistfights. The first small group of us that called ourselves Esther's Follies did our odd mix of intellectual and lowbrow cabarets during the wee hours when respectable people were home watching late-night TV. We amused ourselves with live readings of comic books, reworked renditions of songs from the '20s and '30s, or mangled mock ballets. Our performances were so idiosyncratic and under-rehearsed we didn't charge a cent, although at the end of a show we'd pass the hat. At first we were entertaining just ourselves and a handful of other night wanderers, but within a month we found ourselves with a following. Then Jim Ayres dropped by one night to check on the handful of Winedale alumni who were part of the company, bringing with him two free kegs of beer. Our popularity soared. Even the girls from the massage parlor next door started dropping by on their breaks, picking up glasses of ice from the bar so they could soak their aching hands.

Soon the Pool was so crowded we had to start charging admission. Weekend after weekend our popularity grew, and as it did so did the street it was on. From our vantage point onstage we'd felt the changes coming long before they happened. During one rehearsal break, I sat out on the front concrete stoop, sharing a joint with the Follies' skinny, ferally bearded, chain-smoking pianist. We looked around at the sorry stretch of semi-abandoned buildings surrounding us and started to giggle. We were a little buzzed, but we knew in our gut what would happen and we were right on the money. Within a year, that dark street came alight with restaurants, cafes, bars, bookstores, and shops.

The audiences that crowded into the Follies were a mixed mutt of a bunch who didn't just laugh, they roared, and we were sandwiched between them. Instead of a wall behind our stage we had that wall-length window lined with people peeking in, the ones who didn't want to muscle their way through the crowds or who didn't have the two bits to spare. We were surrounded by energy, and that's what gave our shows an old revivalist feel, or so thought my mother when she came to some early performances before we became a business—from the passing of the hat, to the crazies who would suddenly be taken by a fit of the spirit and get up on that stage with us to dance and shout it out, it was the same kind of spiritual communion.

One night at rehearsal we were trying out a song, "Love for Sale," a heartache of a ballad about the down-and-out that seemed to fit the mood of old Sixth Street perfectly. The whole cast was in the piece, even me. We were supposed to be whores, bums, drifters, and the loveworn. I had never been in a musical number before, and I was in a flutter. I only had to pretend to sing, but I wanted to sync my movements to the words and I couldn't follow the words. A black-eyed, handsome Georgia boy with thick eyebrows and an easy grin put his arm around me and said stick with him, he'd help me fake it. We decided to pair up as a hooker and a drunk, he the hooker, I the drunk. We all got up on the stage to give it a try. At first we meant to parody the song, but as Shannon sang, we found ourselves moved by its beauty. When everyone joined in chorus, even I could tell those voices were sweet, with no trace of mockery. I looked into that Georgia boy's dark eyes and saw the same wonder I was feeling—to be up there onstage together in such perfect accord. And I fell in love with theater all over again.

What happened in that space was a true community epiphany, and it made me something of a star. The one who started the star ball rolling for me was my friend Ernie, a tallish man with a stentorian voice, a big, wide torso, skinny little legs, eyes as blue as the water under the ice of a lake, and a beard with the same thickness and shape as the one Michelangelo painted on God in the Sistine Chapel. He was a Follies writer and my good buddy from Winedale, but our history was more involved than that. When I was still living with my parents, he'd drive over, say hi to my family, then climb the stairs to my bedroom. We'd stay up half the night reading aloud from my extensive collection of comic books. We'd divide up the parts and try out a million different voices and then go over to Jo Jo's, where my sister Tenley waitressed, to order a late-night breakfast. Ernie got a kick out of it when I shoved toilet paper up my nose, the better to embody the clueless, bumbling football coach in a *Bridal Romance* comic, and he'd loved watching me clump around the Winedale barn when I played Bardolph in *The Merry Wives of Windsor*, a character very like that dodo comic book coach. Ernie decided he'd write something funny for me to play at Esther's. His creation, Jake Ratchett, Short Detective, was a very film-noirish picture of a tough guy in miniature. *Texas Monthly* called the character "a brash operative who talks like Bogart and looks like Chaplin." It was a role uncannily like my own private nine-year-old drag act. As Ratchett, I not only got to ape Chaplin and Bogart, I got the girl, a tall blond Bacall-ish vamp who was mine for the taking. Shannon, in her red dress, played Rose Simper, the "cheap broad with a record," and every night "I climbed on a chair and took her in my arms." That was my line, and every night in front of several hundred people, who were overwhelmingly more straight than gay, that's exactly what I'd do. I'd climb on a chair, take the tall blonde in my arms, and then our lips would feed hungrily on each other, a comic smooch more like two animals worrying a bone. You might imagine the audience found our butch/femme display mildly titillating, but I never got the feeling they ever really noticed; it was never even really commented on. To the audience and, I have to admit, to myself, I was not a woman in drag; I was the short, trash-talking gumshoe himself. Every Thursday, Friday, and Saturday for a year and a half, our audiences stamped their feet, whistled, and cheered when the Ratchett theme music played, and mouthed certain lines along with us. Offstage they'd buy me drinks, offer me tiny spoonfuls of snortable drugs, grab me in bear hugs, and ask for my scrawled signature on programs or their bared backs. It was heady enough stuff for a little deaf queer to know that a private fantasy turned public had made her one of the stars of her small city. But something even more interesting was happening on the other side of the footlights.

Sex, of course. Not with the woman who performed the divine Rose Simper, but with the woman who embodied the role. This woman was a Texan, and she was all those things I had been taught to think of as glamorous. She looked like an Italian film star, the honey-blond kind. She was known to be sexual, although she was not known to fuck girls. She ran coke for the restaurateur who kept her. She knew a little something about every kind of drug known to mankind. She played viola. She wore black and fur. She seemed always to be in a state of half-dress. When I first saw her onstage she was improvising some bit about Egypt, inspired, I muttered to myself, by the scent she was wearing. I didn't know what to make of her, even the gay boys seemed smothered in her aroma, so I thought it best to affect a mild distaste. It was easy to fault her for being too sexual. I could tell from the way the corners of her mouth drew down as she spoke that she had a drawl, and her way of moving seemed stunned by all those drugs or recent orgasms and just didn't seem "smart." As a good girl I was almost obliged to be snotty about her.

We'd often pass each other in the narrow hall that separated the stage from the dressing room. I would be in fake stubble, my nose rouged red, my shoes on the wrong feet; she would be in something that showed her breasts. I would have just come from doing a pratfall. She would be on her way up to sing the blues.

The hall where we passed each other by was really just an alley, roofless, hot or cold depending on the season. In the guise of the guy, of course, I'd flatten myself against the wall, offering the female generous passage. She, just as generous in return, leaned in, giving me a whiff of her flesh, a little press of her breast, looking me dead in the eye the whole time, really playing the role. She never smiled. A smile would have been distracting. She wanted me to feel it, the meat of her gaze, all that weighty concentration and predatory charm; and then she'd home in on me—on me in my tie, me in my play-pretend, seeing exactly what game it was I was playing, recognizing it, amused by it. Conqueror. Fearless. Under the starry night. Ironic or not, ridiculous or not, it's a sexy thing to believe.

We both knew the game we played. We both liked playing it and wanted to play it a little longer, a little more intimately. Neither of us bothered to say it aloud. We could both smell it. We were disdainful of talk. Why bother when all you needed was a whiff and a look?

Every look we gave each other was a dare. Play the role out. Take me. Show me how it works. *If* it works. Let's see if there's really anything better about this new way of playing it or if it really is anything new. Because if this new bit of drama was going to be simply business as usual, why not stick to the same old missionary position with the same old equipment? That was the dare. Make me want it. Make it new.

Every breath I took, though, was ragged with terror. She hadn't seen me naked, she hadn't seen me "real." Drag, theater, and play were all helping me to be on top, to be successful, to get the girl. But what would happen after I actually got her, this girl that I had been eyeing from afar, that, in the ordinary guise of myself, I hadn't a prayer of getting, this girl whose body the straight boys wanted and the gay boys faked having.

The first time she and I were together in private it became almost embarrassingly evident how much of our longing for each other had to do with the fictional con-text we were playing in—theater, performance, audience, desire, the heady web of creative complicity. We had not spoken about sex. We had simply gone to her house after a show. We did not take off our clothes. We sat on the floor, stretched out on it, kissed, and instantly we both came. There was absolutely no sex, but there was an orgasm so unexpected and of such intensity that we were both struck dumb.

I had never in my seven previous years of sometimes frenzied sexual trial and error ever had an orgasm like that. But I had no trouble recognizing the state. It wasn't in the least like those other moments when I'd been sud-denly jerked up out of my body to look down upon the world from Olympian heights. I was simply completely, ecstatically happy to be there, completely, ecstatically happy in the moment itself. As happy as I'd felt at Winedale when the temperature dropped and I first lived the word "epiphany."

We stayed together for three tumultuous months as we tried—but never managed—to match the fervor of that astonishing first night. A month into our relationship, she finally told the ginger-haired restaurateur who paid for her apartment, her clothes, and her drugs that we were lovers. He was a Ratchett fan who used her to mule cocaine across the Mexican border, and the only way I could appease his anger and save her job was to cast him in the part of a mob boss. He came to rehearsal dressed to kill, sporting his very own Colt .45. He was pleased to be onstage, and after the show closed that weekend, the three of us vanished. For four days straight we stayed in his upstairs bedroom snorting coke, drinking champagne out of the bottle, and having sex. Or rather, she'd kiss me fiercely on the lips as he entered her from behind while I tried to keep my mind on the passion of it all. Desire with its answering climax had come much more effortlessly to me onstage. Here in the messy middle of two slippery, writhing bodies, far from being gloriously in the moment, I was looking things over with a jaundiced eye, watching the two of them go at it, wondering, *And where do I fit in all this?*

Shhhhhh!

WHEN TENLEY AND I were still little, after Gail had moved to New York and we were left alone with our parents, those two would sometimes disappear together. Tenley and I would be downstairs watching cartoons and then somehow become slowly aware that our parents weren't where they should be—not in the kitchen, not in the back-yard, not on the couch reading. Like ferrets sniffing the air, sensing a coming storm, we'd scamper up the stairs to their bedroom. I'd give the knob of their locked door a hard shake to confirm our suspicions. Then we'd plop down on the carpet and call out in a singsong, "We know what you're doing!" There was never any response that I could hear or Tenley remembers. We'd sprawl on our bel-lies and peek beneath the door to see what we could see, and seeing nothing, we'd stick our fingers under and wig-gle them in greeting. We wanted in on that mystery. I have no idea, never asked our parents, if our games interrupted their enjoyment of each other. I do remember Mother flinging open the door once and barking, "You two!" But then laughing. She was in her long peach robe and when we barreled past her we saw our daddy sprawled out on the bed, dead to the world, a sheet pulled over his body, a pillow for extra protection over his vulnerable midsection. Tenley and I jumped all around the room, pretending to be grasshoppers, then followed our mother into the bathroom as she freshened her lipstick and combed her hair.

A lot of my friends aren't comfortable thinking of their parents as having desires. When they talk about their mothers, the image that pops into my mind is my Granny Doris, hair back in a bun, always in the kitchen cooking up meals for the family or in her living room accompanying herself on the piano while singing hymns in her bright, clear soprano. She died in her sleep at age eighty-six just hours after she had awakened in the hospital to find her youngest daughter, Sue, at her bedside. "Sue," she said, "go on home, honey. I'm having the most wonderful dream." After her funeral, my sisters and I were sorting through a small Whitman's Sampler box full of letters Granny had kept through the years. At the bottom of the box was a strip of four black-and-white pictures in a vertical row, pictures of my grandparents when they were still just Chuck and Doris. Maybe it was simply the contrast—she achingly precise in her light-haired, smiling beauty and he square jawed, with lips so thick their weight pulled his mouth into a scowl; maybe it was how tightly he held her or how deeply she leaned her body into his, but there was no denying it when Gail said, "You can feel the sex between them."

Their daughter, my mother, had been the black sheep of her family, defying church rules that banned makeup and dancing and skirts above the ankles. She married my sexy father at age seventeen, took up smoking, and chose her cosmetics and perfume with care. But still, as a young mother she was none too happy when she walked upstairs into the (aptly named) playroom of our Berlin apartment complex and found me and my friend Billy Lamborn, both of us six, both of us stark naked, pretending to be stage-coach and rider, galloping and whooping, he with a jump rope knotted around his chubby waist and me cracking a leather belt over his head like a whip. I learned my lesson from that bit of interrupted S&M in Berlin. Actually two lessons: avoid public places and keep the noise level down.

Throughout my formative years, as my outward show changed from tomboy to child freak to adolescent geek, I nurtured a rollicking streak I felt compelled to hide. The riper my reproductive system grew, the more dire the consequences became for what I had thought of as a little bit of fun on the side. Nothing was going to stop me from doing what I wanted to do, but it seemed sensible to work out a few hard and fast rules that would keep me from getting pregnant and having to marry or from having an abortion and being jailed. A boy could touch me around the breast but not on the nipple; his penis was allowed to poke only halfway through his pants; he could not kiss me and squeeze my buttocks at the same time; there would be absolutely no sticky liquids and, unless I initiated them, no sudden moves.

Middle school through high school into my first couple of years of college became one extended frustrating bit of guilt-ridden foreplay. At nineteen, in my junior year of college, I was given to wearing long, flowered nightgowns to class and fancied myself an eccentric budding poet à la Emily Dickinson. Being a professional virgin suited me just fine. Then Gail, on a visit home, casually opined that any woman who hadn't lost her virginity by eighteen was doomed to be an inferior artist. I thought, *Uh-oh*. I couldn't even bring myself to insert a tampon. But my sister's word was law: I had to get that hymen busted and fast.

I knew I had it in me to seduce. I'd found that out only a few weeks before Gail's edict, during a weekend retreat of an undergraduate performance class. We were performing in the hill country outside Austin under a warm winter sun. I was in a luscious stage of life, with unblemished, creamy skin, a black cascade of hair that hid my hearing aids, and contact lenses that revealed my eyes to be as hazel as my mother's. I still preferred playing the comic males—contorting my face, getting jerked up by the collar, thrown down flights of stairs—but that weekend the instructor cast me in Marilyn Monroe's role in an excerpt from *Bus Stop*. All a woman has to do in that particular scene is *be*—just sit there and listen. It was the kind of passive girlie role that had once intrigued me but now irritated and bored me, not the least because I couldn't really hear the lines I was supposed to be so fascinated by. But I'd long known that listening can be a kind of rapt attention paid that has nothing to do with the particulars of what's being said, so I decided what the hell. Why not see if I could do it—listen the way Marilyn Monroe had and provoke her kind of desire.

After the stand-in for Montgomery Clift settled his head on my lap, I willed myself to sit still and listen to him, focus every bit of my attention on what he was saying and let the crowd of nine students have their way with me, look their look, feel whatever they were going to feel. I was afraid maybe they wouldn't feel anything at all, but secretly I knew I looked just enough like my mother that they'd feel something, all right, and that made me listen to the man even more intently. There was nothing in the world but the two of us stretched out on the grass, me stroking his temples as he poured out his heart. My lips grew full, my breath slowed. I could feel the weight of his head so near the cleft of my legs, and smell the Irish Spring he'd used to bathe. The more I concentrated on him, the more I felt the eyes of our audience fix on me. The weight of their attention put me in danger of becoming self-conscious and doubtful and I knew if I paid them too much attention in return, I'd stop believing I had the power to do what I was obviously doing. To keep myself Marilynized, I started pretending someone in the audience was in love with me, someone who wanted nothing more than to abandon herself to the longing I was helping her imagine.

I meant to weave the same trance of longing I'd found myself in one afternoon in Berlin, watching my young mother iron. Dressed in her black capri pants, her red blouse tied at the waist, she sprinkled water over one of my father's khaki shirts and began to sing along to music on the radio. As she sang and ironed, the steam rose up around her like smoke around a nightclub stage. I could smell the steam—the moist heat of it made her perfume suddenly bloom. Midway into the song, she caught my eye and dropped her voice. It was just the two of us then. She was confiding in me as she sang, telling me she was falling in love again. She didn't wanna do it, she didn't mean to do it. But oh she seemed to be so happy to be singing about it in that small play she presented to me as she was ironing. And as she sang I was falling in love, too. I was her audience. Enthralled. All hers.

I must have had some of that same effect on my own audience all those years later during that class in the hill country. In the midnight hours after my performance, as the rest of the students in our cabin slept, a former high school beauty queen, aloof, green-eyed, with waist-length, red-gold spun hair, snuck down from the top bunk and slipped into the bottom one where I lay. I came awake instantly. She put her fingers to my lips to signal quiet; then she wrote on my palm with her finger, "I want you."

Her *want* didn't translate into anything more than heavy petting, though. Even if we'd gone farther south, I wasn't sure it would count. During a recent game of Scare, I'd hidden—as had become my lazy habit—between the mattress and the box spring of my parents' bed, where I discovered, to my consternation, a well-thumbed copy of Frank Harris's *My Life and Loves,* which I stole and read. And in that book "sex" was spelled with two *p*'s, as in "penis" and "penetration."

Two weeks to the day of Gail's pronouncement, I corralled the curly-haired Jewish cowboy backpacker I'd flirted with at a Students for a Democratic Society meeting and we did the deed. I was grateful to that sweet boy for seeing me over the hump, but after our short-lived affair I went a little nuts. I decided that in order to become a really great artist instead of a merely good one I was going to have to have every kind of sex I could stomach.

As a consequence, I ended up in some odd beds. And for some reason, known only to the misfiring synapses of my brain, all through that first year after I'd ceased to be a virgin I felt compelled to present myself as one. So it was my maiden voyage out when I bedded the tall, already balding, bespectacled boy in his late twenties who shivered when he nuzzled my naked back but turned into a little shrew when he saw the red Triumph Spitfire my parents had bought me, denouncing it as hopelessly bourgeois even though his dream of a brave new world always involved me typing up his manuscripts. I was untouched territory when the academic couple with the open marriage introduced me to an out-of-town classics professor, his wife, and her mistress, all with whom I ended up in various configurations on the Berber rug during a long, drunken, drug-infused weekend of Roman-themed debauchery. I'd been pure as driven snow before I hooked up with a linguistics professor, a woman from New Jersey who had a hard, wisecracking air and liked to play the man (and had the toys to do it too) during our month and a half of secret encounters, and who couldn't understand it when I walked out on her after she'd backhanded me across the chops. I had to be coaxed out of my tremulous innocence by the convivial lesbian couple who claimed three was the healthiest number in the sack and then, after I'd crawled in there with them, proceeded to squabble about who would go first and ended their seven-year relationship before the sex had even begun.

The whole first year I was hopping in and out of beds, I felt as pitiless and malleable as Bugs Bunny—shotgun-toting big-game hunter one minute; fruit-laden, eyelash-batting seductress the next—all in pursuit of the golden carrot of superior artistry. I labored hard to make my sexual antics heady and exhilarating enough to be worthy of Art. But too much activity in too little time, besides making me bowlegged, was proving to be irksome. I kept thinking that sex play ought to be a joy and—through no fault of my many partners—too often it simply wasn't. My never-ending love/hate relationship with my body just wouldn't allow it to be.

For years I'd despised my body because I couldn't shake the image of it in glasses, hearing aids, and a hairdo that looked like it belonged on Bozo's kid sister. After the hearing aids got small enough to tuck behind the ears and the glasses morphed into contacts, I found yet another reason to hate my body—it still wasn't a boy's, which wasn't so bad when I was frolicking with the men. They seemed to enjoy my womanly roundness more than I did. After I discovered condoms, sex with men was always easy, and I never had to worry or work at it too hard. The women were something else. And more and more often I was finding myself in bed with them. They took work. Especially for someone who had been a failure at masturbation. I thought I could make up for my lack of finesse with sheer aggression, so the minute we'd hit the mattress I'd hop on top and wedge my leg between the woman's thighs and push her up against the sheets, getting a little rhythm going.

Midway into the polka, I'd become aware that the breath in my ear wasn't the random happy panting of sexual frenzy but the cadenced breath of persistent speech, which meant that my partner was probably trying to pass on some urgently needed information. I'd stick my nose under her chin to get at eye level with her mouth, but we were in bed with the lights on dim, not the ideal environment for lip reading. And then, whump. It would all hit me as ridiculous and I'd want to laugh, but sex was just too serious back then. So instead I'd get to thinking what a fucking crap-ass lover of women I was and that would bring things to a screeching halt. The women usually took it in stride and would roll over like buoys in water to pop up on top and get things going again. Even in my brief encounter with the green-eyed beauty queen, I'd ended up the bottom. I reasoned, in the insane logic of that time in my life, that if I was ever going to attain top-dog status in bed I was going to have to get more boy-like, rid myself of my cumbersome breasts, my curvy hips, and my moon of a butt. Drastic measures would have to be taken. I was going to have to starve my uncooperative female animal body into submission.

Body issues have a long history with the women in my family. When my Granny Doris was in her mid-eighties she became seriously ill and lost about fifty pounds. Her body stood the weight loss well and in pictures of her at the time she looks curvy and appealing. When Doris saw one of those pictures, she shook it in her fist and said, "Look at this. It makes me mad. I have to be old as the hills and sick as a dog to get a figure this cute." My mother, Edna, used to eat a piece of half-burnt toast with a little bit of butter for breakfast. She took her morning coffee creamy and sweet. For lunch she'd eat Campbell's vegetable soup right out of the can. When she thought she was getting too fat she did the same for dinner. Every night before bed she did sit-ups and leg lifts. She took up smoking when she was seventeen to look sophisticated, to help her lose weight.

I had already instituted my own practice of weight control when I was eighteen, after reading an intriguing chapter on the Romans and their vomitoriums in a book about the decline of Western civilization. Thereafter, whenever I'd get anxious about the number of calories I'd downed at dinner, I'd excuse myself, rocket upstairs, poke my fingers down my throat, and zip back downstairs before anyone else had left the table. If someone got nosy about my sudden departures, I'd crack a private pun and answer, "Something came up." Bulimic purging was an occasional thing to do. But after I started my sybaritic sexual explorations, vomiting became an almost constant after-meal habit. If I was feeling really anxious I'd vomit breakfast, lunch, and dinner. I was caught at it only once. I was spending the summer in my parents' two-story home in South Austin, where I'd set up shop in the walk-in closet of my old upstairs bedroom. It was more private there, unlike the bathroom, which in our family was like Grand Central Station. One afternoon after downing a half-quart of ice cream and a sack of chocolate chip cookies, I retired to my closet. On the floor, covered by my dirty clothes, I kept a big ceramic bowl. Tucked away on the upper shelf among my sweaters was a long wooden cooking spoon, because my finger no longer worked to make me vomit. Tenley had been looking for me, but I was nowhere to be found. She took advantage of my absence to sneak into my room to borrow one of my granny gowns. She opened the closet door and there I was, hovering over a ceramic bowl, a wooden spoon stuck down my throat, vomit dripping from my chin. Furious that I hadn't heard her coming, that she'd stumbled upon my secret, I looked up at her and snarled. She turned on her heel, leaving the door wide open, and went down, I was sure, to tell Mother. As is it turns out, it stayed our little secret. Tenley never said a word.

I was keeping other secrets from my family which I thought were much more shameful. My entire sex life, for instance. It strikes me funny now that of all the things I was doing then—the threesomes, the foursomes, the sixsomes, with the tinker, the tailor, the mescaline maker— the one thing I dreaded my parents discovering was that I was sleeping with women. Now, my parents were New Deal Democrats, staunch believers in civil rights, who grew more, not less, liberal the older they became. Yet I was sure that if I told them I was having lesbian sex they'd disown me. I'd never forgotten the commotion I'd caused as a preteen when I'd brought up the word "homosexual" at the dinner table. And even though times had changed, I knew my father during his years as a spy had been indoctrinated to fear and hate gay men, a fear and hatred I thought might spill over onto the queer women. As for my mother, she enjoyed hearing about the antics of Gail's former roommate in New York, a tiny blond male dancer who wore long, Isadora Duncan—esque scarves and was given to dramatic meltdowns. But I had a feeling she wouldn't be so tickled by stories of my own escapades. It seemed smarter to keep mum. Besides, I was sure the lesbianism, like all the other sexual experimentation, was like the bulimia— a passing thing. Then it became more than a passing thing.

She was a French woman living in Texas, although there was nothing to mark her as French other than her good, strong nose and the decisive way she had of snapping, "*Non!*" She'd come to a poetry reading where I was the featured reader and invited me to a party at her female Spanish lover's house. In no time at all we ended up in bed in my new brick studio apartment. Her Spanish lover made an appearance around 2 a.m., banging on the door so hard even I could hear it, screaming thousands of colorful invectives that I couldn't hear and wouldn't have been able to understand if I had. Drama, it seemed, was not only the way of the artist, it was the way of the French and the Spanish. Right there in the doorway those two had what looked to be a bilingual conversation so intense I was sure it would end in a gunshot. It ended in a weepy cordiality. They were destined, they had decided, to be friends, not lovers. No hard feelings. "I forgive you your treachery, my compadre," her lover said. "But I spit on the grave of the deaf one." Or at least that's what it looked like she said before she slammed the door with a bang and peeled out of there.

We were both feeling a little shaken by the encounter, and at six that morning we went to the Steak and Eggs and ordered steak and eggs. We sat there and talked. It was one of the first times I had actually talked with someone I had fucked. Her name was Isabelle. And I was stunned by what I'd done to her. I knew she had a real relationship with that other woman and I was ashamed not just of having broken them up but of having said the word "love" to her at one point during our fucking, because I wasn't at all sure I'd meant it. It was just a seduction technique. I started to weep, because if indeed I did love her then that meant I was a lesbian and I wasn't sure I had the guts to be one.

I was so afraid someone might suspect that we were "together," I got knots in my stomach just sitting side by side with her in a booth at the Steak and Eggs. Whenever I'm nervous I talk. A lot. I started telling her about the lesbian couple, the convivial, squabbling one with whom I'd been casual friends until that ill-fated night. And how their idea of foreplay was to put pressure on me to declare myself one way or the other, which I did with the same evangelical fervor with which I'd been baptized as a child, when I was being baptized at a different church every month because the spirit kept moving me into crushes on many different proselytizing cute little Christian girls who were just as earnest as the lesbians in wanting to save my soul. And then, scarcely pausing for breath, I admitted to her what seemed to me my most shameful of shameful secrets. Not the bulimia. The time I went to view a duplex for rent and ended up dry-humping the yummy-smelling male real estate agent on the counter of the empty kitchen, and then ran over to the house of those two lesbians and wept that he'd forced himself on me. When one of them said the word "rape," I came to my senses and tried to recant. But they weren't having any of it and insisted on calling the law until I said, "Look, I'd have to tell them *I* raped *him*. I was the one who wanted it. I was the one who pushed him up against the wall à la *Last Tango*!" They looked at me in a new, uneasy light—*I'd* been the aggressor!? Ahhhh! What to make of that? Then the whole thing dissolved into a pulled-together dinner of leftovers that culminated in the botched threesome.

"So you see, Isabelle," I said, "I'm a bogus lesbian, a bisexual snake. And a nasty little liar to boot. Flee from my company." Which was what I fully expected her to do, but she didn't. She just looked at me a moment and then said something in what had to be French because her lips barely moved—words that could have meant anything but I took to mean, "Wow." But I couldn't leave it at that. I told her I hadn't been joking when I'd admitted sexually adventurous old me was terrified of sitting side by side in the booth the way we were doing because I really did fear the waitress might get a whiff of our same-sex corruption and call out the dogs. Rather than have me committed, Isabelle smiled, stood up, and parked herself across the table, saying, "These things take time." I wasn't prepared for kindness. I wasn't prepared for her to let me off the hook, let me drop the pretense of being erotically in the know, let me admit I was feeling adrift and scared shitless and that I didn't really know what love was.

We were lovers only three more years after that night
—from the time I was twenty-five until I was twenty-
eight—but have remained confidantes and neighbors over
the decades. Even though it was our eventual destiny to
be friends, it was Isabelle—more than any lover but the
one I am with now, the one I've been with for over twenty
years—who taught me the intricacies of true devotion.
And yet it was Isabelle with whom I lived during those
early years at the Follies. She who was then my friend,
lover, and collaborator. And she whom I betrayed during
my astonishing night of ephiphany when I reached orgasm
without even having sex and was so completely, ecstatically happy in the moment.

"Betrayed" is such a loaded word. Isabelle and I had already taken our destined steps toward friendship before
that particular night. And Isabelle had been as intrigued by
the honey-blond vamp as everyone else in the Follies and
would become as deeply fond of her as I was, after finding out, through day-to-day association, that the sex bomb
kept three well-fed, affectionate cats, liked to read quasi-
religious self-help books, brewed up strong pots of tea,
sprinkled cayenne pepper over all her salads, and that she
was as warm, off-beat, and quixotic as the house in which
she lived, which was crowded with antiques, lamps draped
with scarves, and filled with a heady mix of incense, mari-
juana, her aromatic Egyptian perfumes, and the southern
buttermilk biscuits she loved to bake. Isabelle was devas-
tated when that woman and I finally broke up. Saddened
when my next relationship failed. Perplexed when the one
after that bit the dust. Happy as a lark when the following
one went kaput. Philosophical about the next few hundred.
And relieved when it seemed I'd finally settled down at

last.

As for my parents . . .

I lived with my parents off and on until I was twenty-five, and even then I didn't leave home. Home left me. By the time I'd hit twenty-three, both my sisters had married and were living fulfilling lives of their own. My father had moved to Dallas, where his job with the Office of Economic Opportunity had relocated. For two years my mother patiently waited for me to take flight so she could sell the nest and join him. I showed no sign of budging even when my comings and goings made home a closet for quick change. My mother was lonely for her husband, and their long stretches of time apart were making her uneasy. So one morning the suburban family manse was sold. And I was on my own.

That sounds too abrupt. To put it in perspective, by the time I was twenty-five I had been only sporadically employed. After my parents sold their house, they set me up in a brick apartment and gave me a credit card to pay for my meals. They would pay down the card every month until, they said, "I got settled." My experience with money was limited, with credit cards it was null. My idea of responsible debit holding was to treat all of my friends to dinner out. The credit card was quickly rescinded. They still paid for the apartment. I worked odd jobs to pay for everything else.

It was around that time that Isabelle and I became an item and married our fortunes together. Neither of us had much. I'd been let go from my latest job but had the apartment. She had an old Peugeot and a job in a cheese shop, Quel Fromage, where she got me hired on as an assistant slicer. By this time, my parents had taken the extra money from the sale of their house and put it into twenty-six acres of tree-shaded land right outside Austin's city limits. On that land there was a little house, a wooden, gray-weathered pre–Civil War era structure that my father spruced up enough to make livable. He and my mother would commute from Dallas on weekends, and Friday through Sunday, mother would sweep the dust that constantly seeped through the old floorboards while he consulted books on laying foundations, installing electrical wiring, and the how-tos of basic construction as he set about building from scratch the house of my mother's dreams.

Isabelle and I often invited ourselves to dinner there on weekends. My parents were pleased that I had made such a responsible and helpful friend. Neither of them had a clue until I finally couldn't take their oppressively cheerful acceptance anymore and blurted out the awful truth to my mother and Tenley (who'd come to visit) in the parking lot of a Safeway grocery store where we'd gone to stock up for three days of meals. Tenley was gleeful! She'd known it from the start. My mother was surprised into silence. She had never once suspected I was gay. How could I be when I was a tomboy just like her? My mother, like my father, simply thought of Isabelle as an exceptionally close friend. When we got back to the ranchetta my mother immediately went in to rouse my father from his nap. I stayed outside, sitting on the hood of the car until Isabelle came out, *Alfred Hitchcock's Mystery Magazine* in hand, to see about all the commotion. Tenley hugged her tight and told her not to worry, as I broke into dramatic sobs, shrilling, "I told them! I told them!" as if I'd confessed to a spree of serial murders. Then my father stepped outside with my mother and said, "Isabelle, we love you. You are always welcome in our home." And Mother hugged us both.

I was and I was not amazed. Their reactions were everything I'd hoped for. But again, I wasn't prepared for kindness. By then I had heard some pretty harrowing coming-out stories. The diminutive sometime drag queen describing how as a teen he'd been hustled off to a psychiatric facility for electroshock to set him straight. A divorced mother of two weeping over losing custody to her shit bully of a husband after she had a brief fling with another woman. The skinny pianist, tears pouring down into his beard, as he described his fundamentalist parents hissing that he'd been possessed by the devil. I'd been made well aware that the general cultural attitude toward gay men and women in America during the 1970s was every bit as virulent as its attitude toward blacks all the decades before.

My parents were, as I said, on the liberal side of civil rights. My mother doesn't remember any evidence of racial hatred in her own family when she was young. But then of course, she says, "There weren't many blacks in the hick towns where I grew up." My father, an Alabama boy, remembered racism all too well. His family were hardscrabble, hardworking people, most of whom labored in the cotton mills. He loved his mother, three brothers, and five sisters, but when he was in his early twenties, their hard-eyed hatred of "niggers" drove my father from their company. He was a kindhearted, logical-minded boy who excelled in chess and languages. The older he grew the more the unquestioning bigotry of his family perplexed and repulsed him. That's one reason why he and my mother made infrequent trips to Reeltown, where his own mother lived. During a hot summer drive after one such visit, as they were heading back to D.C. before leaving again for Germany, my mother saw an elderly black man who looked shaky and done in by the heat walking by the side of the melting asphalt road. My father pulled over and asked the old gentleman if he'd like a lift. My mother says the offer terrified the man. "Oh no, sir," he said, backing away from the car. "I can't be seen in no auto with white folks, sir. Don't ask again, sir. Please."

"You wouldn't believe how they treated blacks back then," my mother said. "The same way they treated women. The first time we went to visit your daddy's family in Reeltown, I'll never forget it. The women had cooked up a meal and the men came in and plunked their butts down at the table while the women stood up against the walls, their heads down, waiting to serve. I wasn't having anything to do with that. I just sat right down and started to eat."

But the habits of my father's youth were harder to break than he cared to admit even to himself. Early in his career, when he was stationed in Stuttgart, an African American man in his unit was promoted to officer. "I was happy for him," my father said. "Everyone knew he deserved it, but no one thought he'd get it. When he came back into the office, he held out his hand for me to shake. And I shook it. But then—and I didn't even realize what I was doing, it was so ingrained—I wiped my hand off on my shirt." My father's shame was instant and all encompassing. And when I look back on his life after he left the military, it almost seems like atonement for that act of reflexive disdain. Getting his degree in social work. Throwing himself into civil rights. Getting a job with the Office of Economic Opportunity, where he helped minority women get the benefits they deserved. Mentoring a young African American man who worked with him at the OEO, a man who over the years would become closer to him, my father told my mother, than the brothers he loved but felt compelled to distance himself from.

It took me years before I knew my father anywhere near as well as I know my mother, and had I then known his capacity for change, perhaps I wouldn't have been so surprised by his gentle reaction to my queer unveiling. Or been so happily taken aback when he and my mother became close friends with the dark-eyed Georgia boy who had taken me under his wing during my first musical role at Esther's. At some point during my early years at Esther's, every single member of the troupe ended up out at the ranchetta, even the vamp, who, chauffeured by Isabelle, arrived one evening dressed in her usual black, pearls and furs, zonked out of her mind. When she was introduced to my mother and father she gave my mother a too-long hug and my father a sloppy kiss on the corner of his mouth, then went into the back bedroom and collapsed. My parents knew by then not to ask.

Joe, the boy from Georgia, came out with me one weekend and hit it off with my parents so well that he came back the weekend after without me and stayed up all that Friday night talking politics with my father and smoking Winstons with my mother. He was the only one who could ride our wicked chestnut filly, Jezebel, and one of the few my father trusted to help hang sheetrock in the new house. Joe was the son my parents would have loved to have had, the one I'd wished I'd been. A year or two later he and I had some serious talks about having a baby together, talks that thrilled my parents, that's how close those three had become.

It was a good thing we didn't make that baby, though, because just a few months after our procreative discussions, Joe, who was bisexual and made no bones about it, was diagnosed with AIDS. Joe's parents, hearing the news, advised him not to bother coming home. My parents, hearing that, wrote to say he would always have a home with them. Joe, who was living in New York at the time, called to say he loved them and hoped to get back soon to "the pretty little farm where you live." He died four months later of immune thrombocytopenic purpura, bleeding to death in a hospital in Brooklyn after his body began destroying its own platelets. His male lover turned friend, who was with Joe as he died, told me that the last call Joe made was to his family. His mother wouldn't get on the phone, but his father talked with him for over an hour. When finally Joe grew tired, he ended the call, saying, "Daddy, I love you. And that's all that really matters." He would live only twenty-four hours more. My parents grieved for that boy as if he had been their own. Months after Joe died, Tenley came out one weekend to help my father hang the last of the sheetrock in the upstairs bedroom. They were taking a water break when out of the blue he said, "I used to hate gay men. That's what my job required. But I could never hate Joe. It's a prejudice. Like any other."

Jobs for the Deaf

I'M A LITTLE TOUCHY about all the reasons I've spent most of my life being gainfully unemployed. They are myriad and seem to change with the decades. For instance, now I'm woefully out of pocket after three straight years of being flush. It isn't because I can't work. It's because the issue of work is a fudgy one for me, as it's been for a lot of my disabled friends. It sounds ridiculous these days, but in the 1950s and 1960s, on through the decades, the disabled, like women, queers, and people of color, were considered inferior citizens, untrustworthy and incapable of doing anything but scut work. Attitudes change. Kind of.

My first few years after college, when I was without purpose, I fell into jobs more by accident than intent. For periods stretching anywhere from a few weeks to a handful of months I worked variously as a cut-and-paster, an illustrator, a historical archeologist. During that time I also mounted an exhibit of some drawings and paintings that let me support myself for half a year without cadging money from my parents. But after I helped found Esther's I got a taste of what it was like to make a living doing what I loved. My salary from Esther's (such as it was) reinforced my belief that in theater I had found my calling, even if it might be calling me to my doom. When I parted ways with Esther's (we split over, I can hardly believe this now, the use of the word "fuck," of which I was highly in favor), I was too spoiled to consider any life but that one—writer, director, performer. Too bad for me that I was looking for those jobs in Austin during the late 1970s, when there were very few writing, directing, and performing jobs.

During my last years in Austin, in the time-honored tradition of artists everywhere, I took on a series of temporary jobs. Aside from the aforementioned cheese slicing, I worked as a dishwasher, busgirl, poet-in-the-schools, prep cook, children's TV series writer, and house painter. I was also a waitress for all of five minutes, a restaurant hostess for all of ten, and during one particularly lean winter holiday season, I was offered and took a job as an alternative mall's alternative Santa Claus for reasons that had nothing to do with my weight, thank you.

My careers as waitress and hostess were short-lived because, one, I couldn't hear; and two, I couldn't add, and that was too bad, because at the time I really wanted to move up from prep cook/busgirl to the glamour and high tips of waitressing and hostessing. I knew my first stint as a waitress was going to turn out badly the minute I gave the diner at the first table a menu. He had a beard and mumbled, which doomed my understanding of him from the get-go. I made him mime his order.

I might have made it as a hostess if it hadn't been for people phoning for reservations and the fact that I couldn't make change. I had mild success working as a prep cook in a seafood restaurant called Mama's Money until our regular hostess took sick one night and the owner brought me out of the kitchen and put me up front, because the rest of the kitchen crew were mostly ex-cons and they all looked a little scary. "All you have to do is stand there and seat people as they come in," he said. He didn't mention that I'd be answering the phone or I would have clued him in on the oil/water relationship between the deaf and what we call the instrument of doom. He also didn't suspect (because why would he?) that I'd taught myself math and got it all wrong.

The minute he left, the phone started ringing off the hook and a horde of diners descended on the register demanding to pay their bills. I turned off my hearing aids to drown out the ringing while I tried to figure out 20 minus 15.32. I finally threw in the towel and announced we'd be operating on the honor system and they'd have to take their change right from the till. I filed for unemployment the very next day.

To some people, my deafness-induced lateral lisp makes me sound vaguely foreign. This can come in handy when I need to be elusive or mysterious or get myself out of a jam. Only once, however, during my stint as Santa in the alternative mall, did my lisp come in handy on the job.

Once upon a time, being alternative meant makeshift, and true to form the alternative mall that hired me had no ready-to-wear Santa suit I could slip into. It was left entirely to my discretion as to how my Santa should dress. Living in Austin influenced my fashion direction, and I pulled together a red-hotter-than-hell-chili sweatshirt with matching red pants, red-checked bandana, black cowboy boots, and a black toy holster with two six-shooters. My only concession to reigning tastes was the usual stocking cap with its white trim and ball. I stuffed my belly and my bottom with three feather pillows and, voila. Well, voila except for the beard. I emptied three aspirin bottles of their cotton. Being a theatrical sort, I always had spirit gum handy, so I was able to fashion a Santa beard that was entirely, more or less, convincing.

Good as I looked, I felt something vital was missing. Reindeer. I thought *reindeer* rather than *elves* because I had two pair of foam antlers still in their cellophane, which I'd meant to give to the neighbors' two dogs, but a UPS truck had whacked the Chihuahua and the beagle was grieving. My two best male friends, also made gainfully unemployed by the split at the Follies, were easily reached at the local gay bar. They were by that hour in the mood to cavort and didn't notice, much less mind, the foam antlers I affixed to their heads, and they positively adored their jingle-bell bracelets. They balked only upon discovering that as reindeer they were required to cart Santa around the mall in the red wheelbarrow Santa had just dug out of her landlady's garage. The spirit of the season and a second round on me worked to overcome their reluctance, and we headed for the mall.

The manager was due to meet us at the entrance to give us his blessing and the bags of candy we were to bestow on the milling crowds, but he'd been caught up in a merchandising crisis on the second floor and sent the first assistant manager to greet us instead. The first assistant manager seemed to not quite understand our personas or our purpose and was reluctant to part with the bags of candy. I could tell he was embarrassed or at the very least unsure about the effect of our upcoming performance. In retrospect I'd say he was right to be unsure, but still, I reminded him as I grabbed the candy bags, this was an *alternative* mall and it was his boss who asked for an *alternative* Santa and there was no denying I was that.

"The Prancers," as both my reindeer demanded to be called, were suffering an excess of enthusiasm for their newfound roles. They were high-stepping like colts at a derby. They'd issue challenging jingles, paw the air with their hooves, then butt antlers in a mock tussle for dominance. By the time I got them settled down, the boys were feeling headachy and plenty thirsty, so we zipped through that mall in record time. I knew I was tossing the candy far too hard—the shoppers were shielding their faces with their arms—but that was because we were moving way too fast and none too steady, a red feverish blur of jingling frenzy, punctuated by my own shrill whoas of alarm as the wheelbarrow tipped and swerved. We had no Santa village where we could take refuge, so we took a detour outside and came to a wheezing halt near a concrete ashtray so my reindeer could grab a couple of puffs.

There was a child in the vicinity. I thought, *Now's my chance.* I let rip with a few jolly *ho*'s and took a step toward him. I am told that children often cry when confronted with Santa Claus. Maybe it was my fast-disintegrating beard. Maybe it was the pillows slipping down my thighs, giving me an odd *Elephant Man* misshapenness. Maybe it was the specter of the two red-eyed muscle deer behind me, blowing smoke through their noses.

Whatever the reason, the child I approached made not a squeak. I smiled reassuringly at his mother, who seemed herself a tad uncertain. I squatted down to put myself eye-to-eye with my intended audience and said, "Anything you'd like for Christmas?" Those were the magic words.

He was five, maybe six, and he had some serious things in mind to ask for. He poured his little heart out to me. At the end of his lengthy recitation he looked in my eyes so trustingly, so expectantly, I knew he'd just said something that demanded a reply.

That was the glitch I should have been prepared for but alas was not, because in this job like every other, my disability had again taken me by surprise. Deaf as I was, I hadn't understood one word that little boy had said. A list I could handle, no problem—just nod and say yes yes yes. A question was something else again. I was completely thrown, and that triggered a lot of nervous *ho ho ho*-ing on my part. Whatever it was he had first asked me, he asked again. I made what I thought were generically reassuring gibberish noises, but even that didn't satisfy him, so I tapped at my wrist, where there was no watch, and started backing up. For once I was grateful for my lateral lisp, for in it lay the only possibility of escape. "Ah, but you theee," I said, laying it on thick, as I disappeared into the smoke clouds of my reindeer, "Thanta, she hith French!"

The Shallow End

THE THREE YEARS I TOURED with New York's funky Performance Space 122 during the mid-1990s, I was as professional as I was ever going to get. The tours were called the Field Trips, and they were kind of like the vaudeville traveling shows of old, an eclectic mix of different kinds of performances. Only, instead of having a musician blowing smoke rings though a tuba while tootling "Toot, Toot, Tootsie," for instance, we had three blue-faced guys expelling mashed bananas out of tubes hidden under their jumpsuits. When the Trips reached England, all the performers were asked to do workshops in their area of expertise. The three guys did one in drumming with paint, the operatic visual artist did one in voice and spectacle, and I was asked to do a workshop in performance for people with disabilities. It was blithely assumed that being deaf somehow uniquely qualified me for this task. It didn't. I was just as clueless about disabled people as the rest of the world, and shared the impulse to raise my voice and over-enunciate when I encountered someone who was blind, to pat a little person on the head, to pinch the cheek of some brave soldier of a forty-five-year-old businesswoman in a wheelchair. And I was resentful at being assigned an *inferior* workshop.

My group met at a cinderblock community center in a room that doubled as a chapel. I went in there thinking I don't know what—that we'd start by doing some stretching exercises, then play some of the standard theater games I'd picked up by then, like mirroring or body shadowing, some easy physical fun, and then move quickly on to the main event, which would be performing the short scenes and skits I'd brought along with me. Just get in there and get out.

There were fifteen people waiting for me. Among them: a fifty-six-year-old man who had suffered a massive stroke that left him with a constant drool, a dragging foot, and a precarious sense of balance; a thirty-five-year-old former dancer who was in her sporty-looking wheelchair because a drunk driver had barreled over a curb and clipped her in the hips; a forty-year-old woman whose eyes were milky-white from glaucoma; a twenty-six-year-old man who'd lost half his brain in a car accident when the stick shift speared his forehead; and two Down syndrome adults who must have been in their mid-sixties but who were the size and of the mind of seven-year-olds. They were twins, brother and sister, and like me were curious about the long black curtain that obscured the back wall of the room. When we opened the curtain to reveal a pulpit and a cross, the twins fell to their knees, crossed themselves, and began to pray.

If you can't get out of your chair or lift your hand higher than your waist, you can't do the physical games I'd been taught to think essential to theater practice. So I was deciding, as the twins were praying, to skip that part. I wasn't that good at those body warm-ups myself. This group would never miss them, and what did it matter anyway? I said, "Why don't we just read some of these scripts aloud." Even as I said it I realized that half the people in the workshop couldn't speak above a whisper or didn't have the strength or physical skill to hold the scripts or the cognitive skill to read at all. It brought me up short. I floundered around a bit, shuffled through my bag, and then said, "You want to just talk?" That's what we did. For two hours we sat around in a circle and swapped life stories or, in the case of the twins, imitated birds and sang a song their mother had taught them when they were toddlers.

I'd gone into that workshop feeling so superior, so condescending and dismissive. I couldn't imagine that crowd of cripples being anything other than a punishment. And it had gone OK, better than I thought it would. But it didn't much matter. Later on that night, hours after the show, back in my frigid bedsit, picking at the remains of my take-out falafel, I found myself in an anxious sweat. Not over the workshop. Over a memory from Lions Camp for Crippled Children. Talent Night.

Talent Night took place in the camp cafeteria on a Wednesday, so early in the evening it ought to have been called Talent Late-Afternoon. If you wanted to be part of the show, all you had to do was tell the counselor—whom we called William the Blind, to distinguish him from the other William we'd dubbed the Creepy—and he'd enter your name and your talent in his three-ringed binder. All were welcome, talented or not. Now, I have no concept of pitch, note, or tune, and my singing voice is exactly like my father's, who sang pretty much like a frog. But for Talent Night at Lions Camp I'd elected to perform "Sixteen Tons," probably because I knew that only at a camp like this one would I ever be allowed to open my mouth to do more than lip-synch (which isn't something for which the deaf are renowned). I had piano accompaniment, which I couldn't hear, and we lost each other the first few bars of the song. I don't think the audience knew any better than I did when the song had ended, but this was an equal-opportunity camp so I got my round of applause. My swimming competitor, snotty Blind Girl, followed right on my heels. She had, but of course, a pure, true soprano that left silly little smiles on the faces of the counselors. She, but of course, accompanied herself on the piano. My other swimming rival, One Leg, performed a passionate recitation from Shaw's *Saint Joan* for which she received a standing ovation from those of us who could stand. The dwarf played polkas on the accordion that had the whole room a-sway. Some girl named Lois, a heavily overweight, flayed-looking redhead, surprised everyone by gliding gracefully around the stage in an interpretive dance of her own making. With the exception of my performance and the requisite sing-along, it had been a great show.

Remembering that event, I couldn't see much difference between the kids on that stage and the adults who had been in my workshop. I ought to have greeted them as if they'd been my long-lost companions in arms, my Lions Camp comrades grown up. Instead, lodged in my stomach like a sick fear, was the knowledge that when I'd first walked into that space, I had fixed the participants in the workshop with the same blank, negating stare that had so often done me in. Superior. Condescending. Like the snobby once-over I'd endured two decades before when I was at the peak of my happiness at Esther's Follies.

Esther's was midway into its second year of existence when our troupe received a flattering invitation from the wicked old theater department that had once told me no. The department had funds to produce a series of alternative performance workshops and they were offering to pay the writers and directors from our cabaret to devise and conduct three of these workshops. The institution was granting us this boon because we were then drawing audiences that were sometimes larger and definitely more enthusiastic than their own. They wanted to meet with our writer-directors and talk turkey. At that time, Esther's had only two paid writer-directors. I was one and the other wanted to stay home that day and smoke dope.

I arrived at UT with two gay male buddies from Esther's who had come along to keep me company and interpret for me, so I could be sure I understood what was being offered. The young male administrator greeted us all pleasantly enough, but each time he talked business he addressed himself to the men. They were two beautiful young gay men. Worth talking to. He looked them both warmly in the eyes as he outlined all the exciting possibilities inherent in the union between our very successful local theater company and his department. He then proceeded to solicit their input and opinions. Their opinion was that neither of them was either a writer or a director and that he might be better served by addressing me. He was startled by the suggestion. He looked at me and didn't quite smile. "Sure," he said, giving me a nod. Then turned right back to the beautiful boys.

The evening after that meeting I stood in front of a mirror and took a good hard look. I saw how he must have seen me—as a deaf female. Not a big, beautiful, buxom deaf woman who could attract the admiring gazes of straight men. Not a thin, handsome, androgynous deaf girl who might catch the more fanciful eye of gay males. Just an ordinary deaf female. Standing in front of the mirror, I realized I had been naive. In the alternative space I had helped shape, it was a given that my ideas and talents were valued, that I was welcome to participate, to play. Looking at myself in the mirror, I realized that the cheerful matter-of-factness behind that assumption had actually been a luxury, that I had made a grave error by going into that meeting thinking our particular norm was a universal. And I'd been set straight. I had a spectacular haircut, styled just long enough to hide my hearing aids. I picked up the cuticle scissors and started sawing. I was going to give that prick administrator and everyone else something they'd be compelled to look at. And consider. After hours and hours of hacking, I was almost skinheaded. My behind-the-ear hearing aids glinted in the light and at my feet, a pile of dark hair that looked like what it was—a line in the dirt.

Sitting in my freezing room in England all those years later, I felt aghast remembering that act of self-mutilation. I had ruined the last really good haircut of my life. After that sacrifice, how could I have possibly ended up on the same side of the line as that cretinous prick? Especially since I'd run into his kind so many other times in my life since then that he'd become a type, a *them*.

They are as leery of the disabled as they are animals of the wild. They stare, they comment, and when they see us coming they skitter out of the way. They never address us directly but speak to whoever might accompany us, as if we were incapable of reply. If we catch their eye as they stare, their expression is flat, almost sneering, as if they suspected we were faking our disabilities. They just know that the minute their backs are turned the so-called deaf teenager is going to whip out her iPod. To *them* we are the taxpayers' burden, always lobbying for tiny little drinking fountains and ramps, ramps, ramps, and more ramps. They never think twice about parking in a handicapped parking space. In less-civilized countries their kind would whistle cheerily as they deposited the trash—a female or disabled infant—by the side of some less-traveled road.

To another breed of *them*, we are special little angels sent by God to test the spiritual forbearance of the ablebodied. They do everything for us when we let them. They'd happily diaper and feed us whether we needed them to or not. Their eyes well up with tears when they watch us go about our day-to-day lives. Look at how bravely she brushes her teeth! They hold telethons to raise money for our cures, wheeling out the worst-case scenarios for the world to gawk at and pity. They offer to pray to Jesus or Yahweh to cure us of our awful afflictions. They get enormous self-satisfaction from coping with our disabilities.

I had thought I'd put all *them* behind me after I found the good guys, the kinds of people I was fortunate to fall in with at Shakespeare at Winedale, Esther's Follies, and the other alternative spaces that had welcomed me. Those people were funky souls who regarded my deafness (and my queerness, for that matter) as no cause for alarm. Things other than my deafness—my propensity to love everything to death, for instance, or my nasty little temper

—determined if they liked or disliked me. They were usually great believers in democracy and equality, and that, coupled with their profound suspicion of corporate bottom-lines, inclined them to find it more intriguing than threatening that I wanted up on their stages. Their innate curiosity made them willing to help me figure out how to get up there. We figured out really quickly that getting me up there would involve a certain amount of criticism, as hard to give as it would be to take.

If I slurred my words in rehearsal, those guys didn't hesitate to tell me they couldn't understand a thing I was saying. And they'd withstand my rage of frustration after I'd worked for hours in front of a dressing room mirror to get my lips, teeth, and tongue aligned to perfectly enunciate the crucial exit line, only to have the words fall apart like wet cardboard the minute my cue arrived. If I was having trouble figuring out the level of volume I needed to project to the back of a theater, they'd sit in the last row and give me hand signals until I'd hit the mark. And roll their eyes and plug their ears as I panted and huffed, trying to imprint on my brain the amount of air I needed to project the proper distance. If I kept screwing up a cue onstage because it was a line full of *s*'s, *n*'s, *l*'s, and other letters impossible for even the most expert of lip readers to perceive, we'd work out some bit of physical business so I could know a particular gesture signified a particular sentence; or if that gesture slipped by me, whoever was onstage with me at the time would give me a flick, a pinch, or a whack to let me know my cue had arrived. When all else failed and I screwed up onstage, as everyone is wont to do, they treated it as they did any other spectacular fuckup, as a really funny story to be told.

Once (and only once), at Esther's, I was given an actual singing role in an ensemble piece. In the heady spirit of inclusion, I was going to get to sing one line in a skit that the whole cast was in called "Red Sea Story," a parody of the *West Side* one. My line was simple: "I think I'd rather masturbate" (which gives you an idea of the level of humor). It was one line, but a crucial one because it comes at the end of a musical build, like the punch line of a joke. All is going swimmingly, the skit is zipping along, the audience is right there with us, the laughter is building and building. I open my mouth to sing the capper and all that comes out is *gaaaaaaaa*. Nothing more. Everything stops. Every head in the place turns my way. There is a longish moment of thoughtful silence. Then the pianist, bless his soul, startles us all awake with a long, shrill musical trill. And we're back into the song. Albeit another place in the song.

Had there been a lady's razor around I would have immediately taken it to my wrists. To the skit's writer, as to me, it was a failure of catastrophic proportion. To the rest of the cast it was just another occupational hazard. And to the audience? We were doing two shows a night back then. By the second show the place was packed. Word had got round and some people thought the *gaaaaaaaa* was funnier than the punch line. Real moments of personal humiliation. We should have had it on the marquee.

At Esther's and all those other alternative places that had taken me in, we played together with a happy disregard for usual expectation, but always with a longing to reach each other and our audiences in moments of genuine understanding—even if all we were sharing was the thrill of a screwup. How could I have forgotten that generous, if sometimes messy, ethic of accommodation that had welcomed and nurtured me?

In the lumpy discomfort of my English bed, I pulled my coat on over my pj's and curled into a fetal position under the might-as-well-be-nonexistent blanket. Every little shiver seemed like a flick of the lash, just punishment for having somehow become, in the intervening years, another kind of hideous *them*—guilty, as they always were, of an epic failure of imagination. I had failed to understand what I was seeing in that workshop while I was seeing it. The skinny young boy with the hunchbacked shamble, the tubby gray-haired man, his skin puckered by disease, the woman just my age, her eyes disconcertingly whited out. Now I was seeing in my mind's eye those same bodies in the context of theater—bodies that invited stares, whose very presence was evocative, bodies that bucked and shook and seized and couldn't be controlled—and I couldn't help but laugh. When I was doing Shakespeare I'd spent hours applying makeup to get some of those same effects. Those bodies were the very stuff of drama, right there on (what was then) the cutting edge of performance art. I kept thinking of all the other artists I knew or knew of who made a fetish of brutalizing their own flesh—shooting themselves, stuffing live eels down their shirt fronts, screaming themselves silly until their bodies seized or collapsed. I wanted to kick myself. The raw material for performances that in-your-face had been right under my nose.

The twins had come to the cinderblock building in their Sunday finery, he in a dress suit and red bow tie, his hair with a high part and slicked to a sheen, she in a black velvet dress with puffed sleeves, her hair a shoulder-length gray bob held back with a black-and-white polka-dotted ribbon. Those two were memory whizzes, and if you fed

them a few lines at a time they could repeat it letter for letter, inflection for inflection. And they'd remember it for
years. I should have had them try one of the old vaudeville
skits we used to steal and perform at Esther's, like "The
Susquehanna Hat Company." Or maybe a Fanny Brice Baby
Snooks routine. Something from another era, the way they
seemed to be.

The man with the drool and the dragging foot loved
Shakespeare and would have made the perfect Richard III.
It took him a vast amount of energy to get his words out
clearly but he did it. And you could see even as he spoke
how angry it made him to have to work that hard to utter
the simplest sentence. But in his anger there was charm,
and when I couldn't understand the punch line to a joke he
had been telling even after the dancer in the wheelchair had
repeated it for me ad nauseum, he had snorted, twitched at
me with his good eye, grabbed my notebook and pen, and
wrote out the line in laborious hand.

And the dancer herself? Her upper body was nothing
but thick muscle, each arm like the neck of a swan—they
looked as if they could reach and reach and reach and her
hands looked strong enough to snap whatever they finally
reached in two. She could turn her wheelchair in a circle
so tight it looked almost as if she were popping a wheelie.
I'd been fascinated by that chair. I couldn't believe now
that I hadn't tried to do a mirroring exercise with her and
it, tried to follow the mechanical grace of her chair with
movement of my own.

Or the other woman in the two-ton power chair I'd
found equally fascinating. As she sat in its cushions she
seemed frail in comparison to its size and weight, but at
one point—when we had been talking about our secret tal-

ents and what our bodies could and couldn't do—she had half-flung herself out of her chair to the floor to show us how fast she could crawl. "It's not something I do in mixed company," she said, and then scuttled across the room like a crab. What a show we could have put together! And I had blown it.

The people in that workshop knew from my bio that I'd helped found a couple of theaters, gone from stages in Austin to stages in New York, from Lower East Side dives to off Broadway; I'd worked with some famous people, gotten a few things published, and won some grants and prizes. They thought me successful. I was conflicted about what real success might actually be, but deep in my soul I feared not a thing I had done would ever qualify. I owned nothing. I had a bank account of zero, no health insurance, no retirement. Nothing I was doing onstage was going to turn me into an international franchise. But the people in that workshop thought that I—a deaf woman touring with a performance company of international renown—must know something they did not.

Well, I knew something all right. I knew they were idiots to think I had anything at all to teach them. After I'd left Lions Camp, I hadn't gone out of my way to make disabled friends any more than I'd gone searching for deaf ones. In the performance spaces I'd found or helped create I was usually the only deaf or disabled person onstage, and really that had suited me fine. As an artist representative on the steering committee of the National Performance Network, I'd attended a convention of hundreds of performers and producers from all over the nation, not a single one of them disabled. My deafness had made me memorable, and I liked the fuss when people oohed and aahed over how much I had accomplished despite my "terrible handicap." I was made to feel special, a word with which I had had a long and convoluted relationship.

When I was ten, "special" was how my teachers used to refer to me and all the other loser kids with whom I'd been warehoused. But they used it fondly, as if we were big slobbering Labradors they were trying to house-train. In high school I was the one who used the word "special," as in "Well, isn't that *special!*" And if I used it derisively I wasn't referring to the Down syndrome kids but to the stupidly happy middle-class goofs I'd see in TV ads, dressed in matching All-You-Can-Eat Cruise T-shirts, sloshing their mixed drinks while singing "I Will Follow Him." As an adult, "special" had morphed again into a word I couldn't quite despise, because it was a word that was again being applied to me and my talents. Even when it was used to infer that I had been either victimized or spoiled, "special" was the word that got me and my work a little extra attention. I was reluctant to discard it for that reason, but in my gut I couldn't help but resent that word and everyone who used it, because in truth I wanted nothing more than to pass as normal, to jump though all the usual hoops and do what every able-bodied performer in theater could (so I imagined) so effortlessly do. That I sometimes couldn't (and I sometimes really couldn't) made me feel like a cheat. Even with the ethic of accommodation firmly in place, I too often felt about myself the way I felt about the quadriplegic mountain climber who claimed to have conquered the Himalayas. The news photo I saw of him made me raise my eyebrows and click my tongue. It showed him strapped to the back of the man who was doing the actual climbing, and the thought shot through my mind that the more skeptical general public was going to view him as a backpack, not a climber. That's how I felt about myself—as if I'd only been hanging on to people who could actually do theater the way it was meant to be done.

I had been sent to that workshop as a duly appointed rep of disability culture. But that special status had always made me regard my own meager success as being somehow suspect. If those guys in the workshop had been hoping I could teach them new techniques so they could use them to work toward their own measure of theatrical success, it was their crappy bad luck. All I knew how to do was squeeze them—as I had tried to squeeze myself—into the old theater games and practices that were meant for people who, if not always physically beautiful, were always physically intact.

During that restless, freezing night in England, my series of minirevelations had left me glaring at the ugly yellow wallpaper, wide awake and foully irritated. That day's events seemed to be demanding some serious reflection I just didn't have time to give. The Field Trips were moving on the next morning and there was no one to wake me. In college I'd trained myself to wake up without an alarm clock by repeating the magic time like a mantra right before I fell asleep. Usually I'd wake up the next morning at exactly the hour I needed to, but if I were overtired that knack would fail me. I was desperate to put those imperfect bodies out of my mind and put myself on snooze control.

Sure, I could see now how cool it would be, how enthralling and what a fucking relief, to have other people up onstage who were more like me, people who were flawed, people whose badly behaved bodies—like the bodies of the people I had come so close to dismissing out of hand—reflected life as it more actually was. But the whole sticky web of thought was scaring me to death, putting me vis-à-vis that venomous old spider of self-doubt, and my lack of insightful smarts in the face of it was killing me. Nothing I could think or write, nothing I could imagine or dream could put my chaotic thinking to rest, because nothing could uproot the sick feeling, churning deep in my gut, that when I had been sent to that cinderblock building, I'd been sent to swim in the shallow end of the pool.

PART III

Emerging

Scare

I WAS SO YOUNG I didn't even know I was going deaf when I saw a film I thought was about a deaf-blind girl but was actually, I found out later, a silent movie about a blind one. I don't remember the movie's plot, its name, or if the girl had a bit role or was its star. All I remember is the image of her stumbling down a deserted main street, papers and dust in a swirl around her. The look on her face was puzzled and panicked. She knew something spooky was going on but you could tell she wouldn't be able to figure it out quickly enough to get out of the way. There was a tornado tearing up behind her and all I could do was throw popcorn at it and scream at the top of my lungs.

I was a sarcastic little tough of a kid, but seeing that hapless, abandoned child slurped into the funneling maw like a strand of spaghetti awoke in me a deep-seated dread of being left behind when things start going to hell. I knew I could never survive being so forsaken.

Throughout my years that dread has periodically resurfaced to plague me, driving me to have one affair, three drinks, and four snorts too many; and those times when I'd

break down and try to end it all because all was ended, that
dread would drive me straight to the crazy house. Now, I
usually blame everything I don't like about my character
on the twin traumas of my childhood, the disconcerting
deafness and the disquieting hallucinations. But I think
there may actually be something to my suspicion that if
only I'd grown up with all my senses intact, I wouldn't be
as anxiously needy as I am. Too often in love relationships
I have felt like a neurotic poodle, a squirmy, leaky-eyed
Terri with an *i* who can't wait can't wait can't wait for
her owner to return. I know that yappy anxiety is why,
unlike my sisters Gail and Tenley, who were out the door
and into their own lives by the time they were sixteen
and seventeen respectively, I clung to hearth and home and
Mommy and Daddy until I was well into my twenties. I
never stopped trying to regain my original independence,
though. Once I finally did leave home, after my first pam-
pered year out of the nest, my self-reliant streak reasserted
itself and I never again looked to my parents for financial
support. I looked instead to my Art, my various lovers, and
the U.S. government. My Art and my lovers were fickle
in their assistance. The U.S. government was kinder and
more constant.

For a stretch of about three years, starting when I
was twenty-nine, my love life was flickering like a half-
screwed-in lightbulb, and the only work I could find was
sporadic—grants, grunt work, some occasional writing or
acting jobs, some of them pity work, all of them temporary
and only a handful paid worth shit. After I won a fellowship to study theater arts at Columbia and moved to New
York to be a student again (and move closer to a lover I
was doggedly pursuing), my financial state grew ever more

dire. My daily menu consisted of Cream of Wheat and hot dogs without the buns. I lived in a series of rooms, some without heat, most of them free, all of them small, the smallest a closet with a cot. But as I persisted in my dream to be an artist, even those dinners of wienies and gruel seemed within the imaginary perimeters of romantic suffering I thought every artist, disabled or not, was obliged to undergo. Nonetheless, the hearing aids my parents had bought me six years before were held together with masking tape, and I was hearing in flashes: "Terry . . . truck . . . uh-oh." As if every other word was being censored. I didn't like the idea of public assistance, but I needed new hearing aids. Without them, I was fucked. My poverty, in combination with my inability to understand anything that was being said, was brewing the same kind of cocktail of depression and self-loathing that had landed me in the university clinic whimpering like a sick puppy my sophomore year in college. I had to get two new hearing aids or fix the old ones. My only recourse was the state rehabilitation center, but I didn't think they'd give me the hearing aids unless I presented my circumstances as far more desperate than they were. I didn't strike myself as looking disabled enough to deserve the help. I smoked a long elegant lady's pipe (of regular pipe tobacco). I had a great haircut, a sex life, and interesting shoes. My manner struck me as being too cheery and at the same time too weird. I was convinced that in order to get the help I wanted I'd have to present a very different face of need.

The morning of my appointment, I dressed in the drabbest clothes I could dig out of my closet—not a hard search since, like every other aspiring artist in the world, everything I owned was black or gray. I didn't gel my hair up but let it adhere, naturally, flatly to my skull. I left my contacts in their case, my funky glasses by the bedside, and dug up the ghost of three prescriptions past—a hoot-owl-shaped pair with finger-thick lenses I didn't bother to clean, thinking the scratches and smudges would add to the overall effect. I practiced many faces of despair in the mirror and settled on the one that seemed vaguely baby-seal-like, a look that dovetailed nicely with my decision to exaggerate my lisp. On the way up the steps to the office, I had to forcibly stop myself from limping. While grounded in my personal history, the limp seemed a bit too much. I did, however, indulge in a little of the head swaying I'd picked up from watching Stevie Wonder and Ray Charles.

My interviewer was mortifyingly kind. I think he thought I was a "special" student at Columbia with a learning disability I was trying valiantly to disguise. When I walked out of there, morphing back to my sunny, skipping little self, I did feel a residual bit of shame. But I needed those hearing aids. That's how I thought I had to act to get them. And that's how I got them.

They still didn't keep me from going crazy. Three weeks into my new hearing aids, I had an "incident." I had come to New York ostensibly to study theater arts at Columbia, but really I'd followed the woman I loved. She was nine years younger than I and when I first laid eyes on her heart-shaped face at a Winedale reunion, I told myself, *Whoa.* I knew if we became involved I'd have to be careful—we were at such different stages of our lives. Two nights after that first meeting she invited me and another Winedale ex over to dinner and showed us both the wall hangings and lithographs she'd created when she was eighteen. We, her two guests, looked at the art she had mounted and framed and then looked at each other in disbelief. We knew the real deal when we saw it and it was there hanging on her walls. After the artist and I became lovers she warned me that she'd be leaving Texas soon. She'd applied for graduate school at Tyler School of Art in Philadelphia and once she got in she'd be gone. I should have taken the hint but instead I applied for a fellowship to Columbia, left the life I'd built in Austin (which, to be truthful, was already in ruins), and followed her north like a lovesick malamute.

I wanted a settled life with her. She gently but firmly told me no. She was young and needed time to do more exploring. That year in New York I was more isolated than I'd ever been in my life. New York is a phone town. You don't just go dropping in. And of course in those days I couldn't pick up a phone and call. Not my friends in the city, not my friends or family outside of it. At almost thirty, I was older than the other students at Columbia, and in class I was drowning. Until I finally got my new hearing aids I couldn't hear the lectures and what I could hear I couldn't process. My brain was in such a constant tizzy—worried that I'd fail; worried that I already had failed. I had no money. I had no work. There was no such thing as love. I couldn't see my options clearly and ended up thinking I simply didn't have any. By the time I got my new hearing aids, it was almost too late for them to do any good. I'd already started slipping out of my mind. Everywhere I looked I was seeing signs of the end of days. I'd pick up a paper and it was as if there was a secret language embedded in the headlines always telling me that the end was nigh. The hour 3:30 a.m. became a time of great significance. Exactly why, I couldn't be sure, but the omens were there. What were the omens? Nothing tangible, although I did crack open the Bible of a religion I didn't believe in, searching its pages for words that might save me, and became transfixed by Revelations. I sat in my overheated room that winter night reading it in snatches because I was too fearful to read it whole, and what I did read pushed me into such a frenzy of terrified anger, I'd smash the book against my forehead and scream at it, "Give me a break," and "Oh, fucking please!" Everything I read was telling me the same thing. The apocalyptic passages from the Good Book were simply repeating the message I had already gleaned from newspapers, help-wanted flyers, theater posters, and once, marvelously, an ad for Disney World. *They* were coming. And with *them,* the End. I became certain that someone had snuck into my room when I wasn't there, just to look, just to find out exactly the extent of what I knew so they could put a stop to it. Because what I knew was that the world was going to grind to an abrupt halt. And soon. There were disruptions near Saturn that spelled doom for the earth.

Privately I was going completely bonkers, but publicly my craziness remained contained, until one particularly beautiful Sunday morning. I'd been quietly reading the *Times* over my breakfast of cold hot dog smothered in Cream of Wheat. The world news that day wasn't uplifting. Poverty, betrayal, war, war, war. I found myself becoming fixated on an article featuring interviews with middle-school children who were being grilled about their long childhood histories of depression and their use of antidepressants. The interviewer asked a fourteen-year-old boy why he was depressed. He replied, "Because the world is heading for annihilation, of course. But I have accepted it. That there could be an end to Time." I still had a remnant of my sense of humor and thought, *Hmm. That's*

*a hell of a lot more frightening than Margaret Fuller accepting the
universe.*

I don't know why I thought a dose of natural history
would jolly me out of my darkening gloom. But always before, I'd found comfort in those animals tucked inside their
little glass dioramas. They might have been dead but they
looked safe, stuffed and posed in there, like performers
on a stage. I took the subway to the Museum of Natural
History, got my ticket, and made a beeline for my favorite
display, where it is forever midnight on the Alaskan tundra
and two white wolves, the perfect couple, are caught in
eternal midleap. I always thought of it as a kind of Jack
Londony happily-ever-after. If I had stuck with the wolves
maybe I wouldn't have gone as nuts as I did. As it was,
I wandered over to a Disneyesque little forest scene I'd
never seen before. It was just a patch of grass, a scattering
of leaves, a single tree, and, nestled down in a cozy hollow
of roots, a fluffy brown rabbit. I was taking refuge in the
innocuous sweetness of it all until I happened to notice that
some sick fuck of a curator had taken a stuffed red fox and
hidden it in the leaves behind the tree. I was afraid to turn
away, because I knew the minute I did that that fox was going to leap on that rabbit and that's all, folks. My impulse,
sudden and fierce, was to beat on the glass and scream,
"Run bunny wunny! Oh run, idiot, run." But etiquette and
the museum guard demanded not. I could only stand there
staring at the scene with the same tight look of furious dismay I imagine was on my mother's face when she lived in
Berlin and decided that if the jig was up, it was up; and she
refused to pack her bags. I knew what was going to happen
the minute my back was turned and I knew, too, there
wasn't one damn thing I could do about it.

I identified deeply with that rabbit and fled the museum in a state of galvanized psychosis. I sprinted back down into the subway, dashed out at Penn Station, bummed twenty bucks from a complete stranger, and hopped a train to Philly so I could die in the arms of my former true love, but she was out on a date. A week later, after I'd tried to kill myself just to relieve some of the tension, I was admitted to New York's Gracie Square psychiatric hospital.

The admitting physician, after listening to a torrent of childhood stories about empty suitcases, death-foreshadowing cups of tea, and military-approved fake evacuation plans, not to mention well-intentioned doctors wielding havoc-inducing antibiotics—diagnosed me as a possible paranoid schizophrenic. I was hoping to be sedated out of my misery, but that first day they simply deposited me on a bed in a small, bland room empty of detail where they could keep an eye on me, make sure I didn't do what I told them I'd been thinking of doing and run a knife through my neck. Without drugs it was fatally boring.

Gracie Square was a low-key crazy house, or maybe ours was just a low-key crazy ward. There were no bald, rottweiler-eyed, tattooed guards to hustle us screaming to our rooms. But it wasn't any place I'd go to make friends. We inmates barely even noticed one another as we stumbled around in the fog of our own malaise. The only remotely communal thing that happened during my entire four-week stay was an impromptu performance that came about when the night nurse closed down the recreation room two hours earlier than usual because we, the inmates, had been poking fun at Ronald Reagan, who was president at the time. We'd been watching his Iran-Contra testimony, and even the schizophrenic thought it was a hoot. The nurse was a big old bully of a hard-core Republican who had the power of veto and used it. She switched off the television and locked down the room. The small handful of us dawdled out in the corridor, all of us in our pajamas and robes, which gave it something of a slumber-party air. We decided to entertain each other. The spindly nineteen-year-old with an acne-swollen nose and a head full of hair stiff as a Brillo pad, who had repeatedly (and after hearing his life story, I thought with good reason) tried to kill himself, recited prayers in Latin. The manic-depressive, who looked a little like an African American Emma Goldman right down to the round Marxist spectacles, did a clog dance that would have been like *Stomp* if it hadn't been done in slippers. Someone whose illness and particulars I can't remember recited a couple of filthy limericks, and I did an S&M ventriloquist act. I put a string mop over my hand, called it Mister Handchops, talked with it a bit, then had it go nuts and bang itself on the walls screaming, until I subdued it by beating it repeatedly with my shoe. I didn't have a punch line until the schizophrenic added her two cents. She was a tiny, bug-eyed dishwater blonde who often beat her head against the wall when the attendants wouldn't let her smoke or the voices told her she needed to break out of the shell of her skull. As she watched me whack my hand into submission, she sidled over and gave me what would be my closing line: "And then we both cry. Because it hurts me more than it hurts him." It was one of the more gratifying performances of my life.

I was released after four weeks. I was able to pick my life back up again. I started hanging around the Lower East Side, especially around WOW Cafe, where I'd have breakfast in the morning, get up onstage to read some poetry at night. I fell into bed with a woman who shaved her head and was the kindest soul besides Isabelle I had ever met. When I grew anxious about the world's fate during one of our nights together, she took it in stride and simply said, "I want you to remember that 99 percent of what happens in the world is mundane, not tragic." I put together a whole series of one-woman shows and finally wrote one up for my graduate tutorial that was produced by the Women's Project at the American Place Theatre, won a handful of awards, and was made into a never-released film. And I found love again. With an older woman this time, a no-nonsense professor turned director who had something of the same sharp beauty of my much younger ex. She took me into her heart and into her apartment because she had seen my work and loved it. She was funny and probing and unexpectedly, delightfully prim—but that didn't keep me from cheating on her. When I returned home to Austin for a visit, I went, as my lover suggested, over to the University of Texas to introduce myself to a young graduate student in performance studies whom my present lover had once mentored. I knocked on the door. A young woman opened it up. We looked at each other and it was as if we'd both been thrust into some corny Technicolor romance. Time stood still.

Her name was Donna Marie. Six years my junior, tall, effortlessly beautiful, with all-American good looks made a little less wholesome by a certain wicked light in her gray scholar's eyes. Her expression was expectant. Her long, thick, honey-brown hair was pulled back into a loose bun, a few soft tendrils curling around her temples. We were both smiling in exactly the same way, as if we were about to break into song, although it's a good thing we didn't, since neither of us can sing on key. I introduced myself and invited her to a party that was being held to welcome me back to Austin. I got a bit flustered and asked her to call me. I gave her the number of the house where I was staying with Isabelle, her lover Beatrice, and Isabelle's sister Vivian, all of whom were from the same region in southern France, two of whom still had outrageously magnificent French accents. When I told Donna to call me I said, "By the way, I'm deaf so I won't actually hear you when you call. The friends I'm staying with translate for me. They're French." Which confused Donna mightily. She wasn't sure if that meant they would be speaking French if she called me or if they would translate her English into French for me to understand. But she felt it impolite to probe. We ran out of things appropriate to say but neither of us was quite able to move. Then her office mate hailed her with a question, so it seemed time for me to split. As I walked away I thought, *Hmmm*. And she, as she told me later, couldn't sit still the rest of the day. But we were both with other partners then and had resolved to be good.

Still, I felt an urgent need to see her again. I prevailed upon Isabelle to call Donna on my behalf and invite her to a movie. The call was made in English, much to Donna's relief, and the date was set. I realized I had no car. Another call was made. She didn't mind picking me up. We went to the movie (*The Return of Martin Guerre*) and after that to a crowded, blaring sports bar to talk about what we'd seen. In the dim light, with all the din, I couldn't make out a word she was saying. It tied my stomach in knots to tell her how deaf I actually was. But she didn't seem to mind and suggested we head over to her house, which was quite nearby, and have our beer there instead. It would be a lot easier for me to read her lips, she said. I was going to make some crack about would it ever, but I suddenly turned cautious. I really liked her.

She'd just moved into the house her parents had bought for her. The kitchen wall was painted UT burnt orange. We shook our heads over the decorating tastes of the former owner, that too-obvious Longhorn fan, and sat down at her little card table, which was about the only piece of furniture in the place besides a terrible Naugahyde sofa (which was the first thing I threw out after I moved in). Usually I waited until the third date to mention how many times I'd been institutionalized (two). And at least the fourth before I'd let it drop how many times I'd come close to killing myself (eleven and a half, although most were unintentional and one was halfhearted). But that night I told all. She listened with a bemused look in her eye and then told me about her own mini existential crisis when she was a junior in college, after she'd gone to study theater abroad. When she came back to Chicago from the University of Lancaster, she was tapped to be the bridesmaid in a family wedding, and the tons of food, the tower of presents, just everything about middle America suddenly seemed so excessive it made her tired. She didn't have the energy to go back to school. She didn't want to return to the pool, the tennis court, the horses, and the cocktails on the ten acres of rolling land where her family lived in the suburbs of Chicago. She needed time and the solitude to think. So she opted out of college for a year to live with her older sister, who worked for the Mental Health Association in Texas. For four months, she was a nanny for her new niece. And that's all it took for her to get her mind and thoughts and self together. I was enchanted. She seemed so civilized.

"I wasn't gay then," she said.

"What?"

"Well I didn't know I was gay. I could have easily been one of those women who just doesn't have a clue—the kind who marries, has a bunch of kids, and then wakes up one morning to discover she's a lesbian."

"So what brought about your discovery?" I asked.

"Well," she smiled, and it looked a little taunting. "I fell in love with the same woman you did." It took me a moment to realize she was talking about the professor/director who was waiting for me to return to her back in New York. "But I was young and her student," Donna said. "She turned me down."

All of what she said sounded vaguely familiar. Then it hit me. Donna was the woman my New York lover had specifically forbade me from seducing. I could feel my heart shrink. I had been determined to be good, and this new revelation was making me determined to be even better. I steered the conversation back to the safety of our families, saying I'd love to see any pictures she may have. She pulled out four albums of neatly mounted, meticulously labeled photographs, which, I mentally noted, were in grave contrast to my own twenty-two shoeboxes filled with blurry snaps that I'd shoved into the downstairs hall closet of my parents' ranchetta for safekeeping. For the next several hours Donna Marie gave me concise two-line bios of every single member of her enormous extended Irish Catholic clan. There were many of them and all of them good-looking. By 4 a.m., I thought I knew pretty much every important person in her life that I ought to know, which struck me as an odd observation from someone who was determined to be just a casual movie date.

We'd finished the six-pack and were a little looped and totally exhausted, but she didn't invite me to stay. No particular sparks. And we were being good. She drove me back to my temporary digs in Austin, where I was camping out on a blowup mattress on a dining room floor. As we pulled up to the driveway, I thought to myself, *What a nice woman.* She told me later that that was exactly her thought then about me. We turned to each other in the car to say goodnight. I offered her my hand for her to shake, and then somehow we were kissing. Just one kiss, really.

It was like that old saying about your life flashing before your eyes when you die, only this was a flash-forward. I knew from that kiss that the other relationships we were both in would come to messy ends. And there was nothing we could do about it. I knew that I was going to intro-duce her to my friends Isabelle and Beatrice and Vivian and they would instantly take to her, the way my own family would. That my mother would become so enamored with Donna, she'd dream about her even though she had never before dreamed about any of her own children. I knew we'd be negotiating family dynamics and that I'd end up taking a gambling cruise with her family up the Missis-sippi and she'd spend the night after Christmas with mine watching *Henry: Portrait of a Serial Killer.* I knew that even though we made an unlikely couple, a real Mutt and Jeff, in some ways we were exactly alike. We were going to be together for years on end. We'd live in a modest little cot-tage in a pretty little college town where she would teach and I would piddle and we'd make art together with all our friends. We'd wake up every morning and take our coffee hot and strong with a little bit of half-and-half. We'd have our squabbles, our tragedies, and our extramarital affairs. And I knew, too, that despite all my certainty, nothing was ever going to be quite settled. We both had too much wanderlust for that. But with that one kiss I was absolutely certain that, finally, love would save me. I was right about everything but the last.

It was about ten years into our relationship that I took a teaching job at a certain Institute of the Arts in California, in part because it would look good on my resumé and in part because I wanted to spend time with an old Winedale buddy of mine who'd been diagnosed with AIDS. But I knew I was in for some serious insomnia. I didn't sleep well without Donna, and she couldn't get a leave from Florida State University for those five months. We were in for a bicoastal relationship but without the money to cut the distance down to size.

The building in which I had an office was ugly, like a junior high from the '60s, and my cubicle was way down in the confusing maze of the basement. I told everyone in the department that I was deaf and couldn't hear PAs or sirens so if anything ever came up, I hoped they'd think about me down there. They all assured me that they would never forget a thing like that. If anything did happen I'd be first and foremost in their thoughts. Besides, what could possibly happen? I thought, *Well, a fucking earthquake maybe,* but didn't say it.

Three weeks later I'm typing away in my basement cubbyhole. I see by my watch that it's lunchtime. Out into the halls I go. The basement is uncharacteristically empty. And too, the air is heavy with an unwholesome odor. At this point I'm wondering if the emptiness and the odor are tied to one of the esoteric nonholidays the people in this ironic institution sometimes celebrate, which always seem to involve the cooking of very bad food, when *bang!* a space-suited alien storms the hallway and hustles me the hell out.

An art student, using toxic chemicals for a project, had spilled a bucket of the stuff near an air duct, and since that duct networked through the building, the whole school had to be evacuated. Never in the rowdy educational history of the Institute had anything like this happened before. There were sirens, there was commotion, there were shouted public announcements, there were EPA people swarming the grounds within their little self-ventilated biohazard suits. Everybody in the building had gotten the message and hightailed it out of that toxic soup of a building lickety-split. Everyone, that is, but little old deaf me.

The next day, red-eyed and scratchy-voiced, I go into the administrative office of the school and remind them that I'd been forgotten. They apologize profusely. How very sorry. He thought she would get me, she thought he would, and so on and so on. And it would never happen again. Besides, in all the years the school had been in existence, nothing like that spill ever occurred before. What were the chances of it ever occurring again, huh? Much laughter all around (albeit uneasy laughter on my part). But I convinced myself they were right. What had occurred was a confluence of unlikely events that could reoccur only if heaven was as deeply ironic as I feared. I could turn it into a funny story to tell Donna the next time we talked on the phone via TTY. I trotted back down to my basement lair and burrowed in among my books and papers, feeling once again as snug as Mole in his underground nest in *The Wind in the Willows*.

Three days later, it happens again. Not the same student, but toxic substances again, only this time odorless. And this time it isn't lunchtime. So I'm sitting down there cluelessly, happily typing away, awash in a whole new bath of chemicals. It isn't until I get up to go to the bathroom that I see my friends from the EPA roaming the halls in their space suits.

I would have found the whole thing funnier if it hadn't reminded me of the Braniff Airlines debacle I'd survived not long after I'd been discharged from Gracie Square and not long before I was to meet Donna. That was back when I was the most jittery flier imaginable, always searching to the nether end of my dreams for portents of doom. This time was no different, and as I boarded the plane that Wednesday at LaGuardia I couldn't rid myself of the thought that Flight 19 to Austin just wasn't gonna make it. For once I was right on the money. What I didn't suspect was that it wasn't just one measly jet that was going to nose-dive but the whole damn fleet.

The flight itself wasn't exactly uneventful. Thick rain fell the whole Texas route, and as we approached Dallas, hailstones battered the wings. The plane rumbled and shook, as did the passengers. I felt just like that plate rattling over Señor Wences, the ventriloquist on the old *Ed Sullivan Show*. He spins the plate over his head on a stick while the plate sings in a high, shrill voice, "Eye yam noht afraaaaaaid!"

When we touched down in Dallas I'd made peace with God and had broken out my last bucks for a good stiff drink. And then the announcement was made. What I got in translation from a woman sitting next to me was that we were to leave the plane and take our carry-ons with us. Flight 19 wasn't completing the leg to Austin. Over and out. We got out, with minor grumblings. The weather or mechanical failure or something else unforeseen, but we didn't doubt we'd be taken care of. We stepped into the lobby and the top blew off.

The terminal was a roiling sea of television crews, print reporters, photographers, cops, and thousands upon thousands of royally pissed-off frequent and not-so-frequent fliers. We had apparently been dumped. The flight attendants and the pilots had been told en route from New York that Braniff Airlines had breathed its last, but no one thought to tell the passengers.

It had been less than half a year since I'd been discharged from Gracie Square psychiatric hospital after suffering my nervous breakdown, during which I read into newspaper articles, billboards, passages from books, and scraps of paper just laying around the unmistakable signs of the end of the world. So when I buttonholed one of the stewardesses who was rushing off and asked her what the hell was going on and she replied "Everything's finished, it's over, done," of course I thought she meant the End had come. The thought of spending my last moments on earth in the Dallas-Ft. Worth terminal was not a happy one. I grabbed her arm for support and asked in a piteous whisper, "Are we really gonna die in this godforsaken place?" That's when she explained that no, this was just a big fat corporate death. Then she peeled away and that was the last I saw of her.

The terminal was a madhouse—luggage by the ton

strewn all over the lobby, phone lines tied up (this was before cell phones and text messaging), boiling tempers, frantic husbands, worried wives, and wailing babies. To top it all off, everything had been locked down—even the restrooms. "And where," I inquired of the lone remaining security guard, "am I to do my business?" She directed me to the other terminal many miles down the road. I was nonplussed, and expressed my nonplussedness by heading out into the parking garage and doing something I have never done before or since. I sandwiched myself between two cars, stepped out of my pants, and pissed, rather inexpertly, all over the front grille of the newest, most expensive car I could find. I know it was bordering on nuts, but rich is rich and I knew some rich greedheads somewhere were responsible for this cock-up.

My mind cleared of resentment, I began to plot my escape from Braniff's little economic Saigon. I approached the security guard again. "Listen, I'm a deaf woman who is a former inmate of a crazy house. If somebody here doesn't give me a hand, I think I may just fall to pieces right here in your lobby in front of all those television cameras." I was frothing a little at the mouth and allowed her a discreet glimpse of my trembling hands. Her eyebrows shot up a foot. She collared the woman nearest her and did some fast talking. The woman immediately took my arm and said, "Come with me." A heroic official? Nope. Just another passenger. Thus I came to understand that in times of crisis the victims are required to help each other.

My fellow victim was a twice-divorced sixth-grade schoolteacher from Lubbock, Texas, the mother of three children, one of whom was due for surgery the next day. We shook hands. I explained my deafness and why

I couldn't use phones. She telephoned an SOS to Austin for me, and when her nephew arrived to take her home, we shook hands again and promised to keep in touch. Of course we never did.

I waited there until 4 a.m. Torrential rains were delaying salvation. By that time the lobby had taken on a desolate and surreal air. The Braniff people, along with everyone else, had long since abandoned ship, the storm outside had reached maniacal proportions, and there was only one other companion-in-misery to be found. She was curled up on her luggage and looked more lost than I felt. "Has anyone helped you?" I asked. She smiled shyly and said something in a language I couldn't lip-read. I looked at her ticket. Sure enough. "Speaks no English," it read. "Please give special care."

Half a year earlier when I had first gone crazy with fright, the Gracie Square attending physician had put me on Haldol. When I was calm enough to focus on his lips, he advised me, among other things, to change my reading, movie, and museum-going habits. No more desperate accounts, either fictional or real, of people who couldn't be saved because there was nothing in place to save them— the ones who didn't hear the warnings, who didn't see the flashing lights, who couldn't make it down 102 or even just 2 flights of stairs on their own. Such stories would only serve to stir up unrealistic (can you say *crazy*) fears. I was too emotionally comatose from the drug to do anything but agree and handed over my copy of *The Fate of the Earth* in which all the sentences had been repunctuated with inky exclamation marks and every single page glowed from the yellow highlighting.

The weeks I spent in the nuthouse I worked hard to

build up a sturdy, if cautious, optimism, avoiding books, newspapers, television broadcasts, even casual conversations that might distress me. I did have one minor relapse after I read a back issue of *Reader's Digest* featuring an alarming report about long-distance haulers falling asleep at the wheels of their twenty-ton semis and the driving tricks to avoid them. The day I was released from the Square, I thought I had cultivated an indestructible inner smiley face.

Six months later I stood in the eerily empty Braniff terminal, reading the tag on the abandoned woman's wrist that singled her out for special care. As I read, I could feel all my old panic welling as the most overquoted refrain in the history of poetry came unbidden to my head: "This is the way the world ends." It seemed fitting to whimper.

Twenty-four years have passed since that day. I have long since created a life that surrounds me with as much love as life can muster. But that fearfulness exists in me like a banked fire waiting to flare up with a simple gust of air. I learned from it that nothing in this world, not even love, can save me from the fate that awaits us all. The whole world of us doomed, one by one. That was always my real fear when my mind would slip. And there really isn't one damn thing any of us can do about it. Better to give it a nod and then put it aside for future study.

So at night after rehearsal or after our other more mundane chores are done, I'll stretch out on the futon in the TV room and channel surf, while Donna leans back against my knees, reading some fat, dull academic book. During the commercials I'll comb her honey-colored hair or search her skin for any dark suspicious moles while she rubs my aching knee. And later we'll fall asleep with our little cat Tweety curled up on the blanket at our feet. I may still wake up at three-thirty in the morning—the imagined hour of my grim reckoning—and wait breathlessly for the dread fall. But Donna will feel me rouse, and reach out for me in the dark to pull my body to her own, and stroke my naked back until, at last, I feel safe enough in her arms to sleep.

Who Died and
What Killed Them

THERE IS AN EXISTENTIAL FUNK you can get into when you lose a sense the way I did—uncertainly, in increments, knowing what you're losing even before it's lost, and, as always, wondering why, to what end. It's a process akin to dying, and early in life took away my confidence in a world where things would always work out right. When your body betrays you like mine did me, then who's to say the world won't crack open at your feet, the sea rise up to sweep you away, or the sky rain down its cosmic debris?

I used to think it was that underlying disquiet that provoked my love for the family stories about who died and what killed them. But my sisters and my mother, and my father when he lived, loved hearing and telling those stories as well, so if it's a mental affliction, it's a family one. I'm hoping, though, that what I'm about to admit is something particular to me. During a large chunk of my life, I was almost pathologically obsessed with the deathbed stories of beautiful boys cut down in their youthful prime.

My handsome Uncle Don was much in my mind when I was growing up because, except for the blue-veined baby

Robert, who died in his sleep, Don was the only one of the boys in my mother's family I didn't know. Don and his brother Ernie (whom I do know) were so close in age they might as well have been twins. I used to pore over old high school photographs of the two of them, and it was like looking at photos of movie stars. They both had the soft swollen lips of a James Dean and his same crinkly wounded expression around the eyes. But Don, with his flattened nose and muscled torso, had a touch of Marlon Brando about him. He looked like the tough little cowboy he was. And he did what every cowboy from Graham, Texas, was expected to do—won himself a football scholarship to the University of Texas in Austin. Once there, he became the hero he was expected to become, if only for one game. The details of his football heroics died with my father, who was the only male in our small family. Mother hates football and all she remembers is that Don was coached by Blair Cherry and was a buddy of Bobby Layne.

I do remember Daddy once describing Don's big game. It was a grudge match the Texas Longhorns played in the late 1940s, but I have no idea if the mortal enemy was Texas A&M, Oklahoma, or Alabama. Texas had the thinnest of leads when their rivals got possession with just seconds on the clock. The opposing quarterback lobbed a short pass, the receiver caught it and took off running. He was quick and big and what he couldn't elude he barreled over until there was only one Longhorn standing between him and the goal, my Uncle Don, who at six feet was shorter than the average tackle but so compact and tenacious that his teammates had nicknamed him Bulldog. Bulldog obviously didn't strike fear in the hearts of his enemies, because this enemy didn't even bother to swerve. I like to think he regretted his arrogance when Bulldog hit him straight in the gut so hard it lifted him off his feet before he smacked to the ground. So the game was won and it was my Uncle Don who had carried the day. He never played a minute of professional ball after he graduated, but married his college sweetheart, fathered a son and a daughter, and went on to become a high school coach and an English teacher. By all accounts he was settling down to a perfectly realized and happy life. Then, when he was twenty-seven, he started feeling sick to his stomach. He ignored the queasiness until it changed into an unrelenting ache in his side.

The boys who played football in his day were taught to be stoics. They'd break their femurs and beg to crawl back onto the field. If the pain was blinding but they were still upright, the team doctor would shoot them with a painkiller and push them back in the game. Don got hit a lot, mostly in the kidneys. Just how hard and how damaging became clear when the nephritis kicked in. There wasn't much doctors could do for diseased kidneys then, and what they did do bordered on torture. As the body began to die from the excess of toxins, the physicians would strap off the extremities with tourniquets so the heart wouldn't have to work so hard to pump blood to the brain. The pain of it was excruciating, but Don took it like the sweet-hearted hero that he was, sitting up in his hospital bed, calmly grading his students' essays until the day they tied off the circulation to his arms, which was the day that beautiful boy finally died.

My friend Donald was a different type of beautiful boy. Blond and blue-eyed with a pretty ruffle of hair on his long, sculpted arms, Donald was a poet who had just moved from New York to Los Angeles when he was diagnosed with

AIDS. I live in Florida, but I visited him often, even taking a teaching job there to be near him after his health started to give way. Donald had always fixed a hard, critical eye on the body, his own and everyone else's. And when we were students together at Shakespeare at Winedale he'd join me in critiques of my own flesh, once remarking that my breasts were "withered dugs" and my arms would soon be sagging like "all those dykes who bowl." Even as he was cutting me up, weighing me piece by piece, not just looking at imperfection, but for it, with a studied intensity, the expression in his eyes was calm. We both thought, then, he was only criticizing me because he loved me. If he hadn't, he wouldn't even have bothered to look.

His own beauty and wit had given him entrée to a world I had always envied and always imagined as the source of my self-loathing. I thought of it then as a world populated by nothing but beautiful boys, many who were mentored, fathered, in a way, by beautiful men (or famously talented ugly men). They were all part of a literary network that swapped lovers more casually than manuscripts. My first week in New York, after I'd moved there to study at Columbia, Donald and two of his beautiful poet buddies took me to see the native sights, which to them meant "Donkey Fucks Woman Live!," then showing right off Times Square. Donald had told me to dress in drag, to see if they could smuggle me past the bouncer/doorman at the Anvil, a total sleaze bar where men fucked pretty much without pretence. He and the other two boys were indignant as mother hens when the doorman took one look at me and laughed. He was built like Conan the Barbarian, so there was no arguing with the grunt of dismissal that followed.

For the most part, all those young beautiful boys

were good to me. But there was one, an Alpha gay, who took pride in being a study of merciless detachment, who looked my body over, when we were first introduced, as if he found it hardly worth a sneer. He was wildly influential among his gay male poet peers, as of course he would be—he was well-read, well-heeled, well-traveled, which somehow translated into an imperious impatience worthy of Prince Hal. In his company I squirmed the way I'd squirmed when the theater adviser at UT gave me the once-over right before he told me no.

The older I grew, the more susceptible I became to the sneering once-over, real or imagined. So I was relieved when Donald introduced me to David, a kind, tall, blond man with pretty lips that dimpled at the corners in a way that let me know he was southern. He liked to cook and make things cozy, and Donald called him the love of his life. I was grateful for his company, because, just as Donald tempered his lover's too-soft heart with a leaven of malice, David kept Donald's sometimes too acerbic wit on the funny side of vicious.

The last time I saw Donald, he'd come alone to stay a week with me when I was performing in Scotland. By then Donald was nearing the last stages of his disease and no longer had any feeling in the soles of his feet. That lack of feeling gave him the same heavy off-balanced gait as Mike, the little boy with muscular dystrophy I had known growing up. Donald was still a young man, but when I kissed him hello and told him how happy I was to have him there with me, he looked almost embarrassed, apologized for how scrawny he'd become, told me a quick story about being upgraded from coach to first class most likely because the crew was terrified that he'd die midflight; then he derided himself as "a tired old queer." The first night of his visit we were sharing a sink, washing up, preparing for our night, standing side by side looking at ourselves in the wide bathroom mirror. I turned away from myself to look at the mirrored image of his body dying in front of me. He was very thin, almost cadaverous. But seeing his ravaged body, all I could think was that his face had the starved, sunken look of a saint. I glanced up to see him looking just as intently at me. I still feared his cruel eye. But he said, "Yes. I love you too."

Once upon a time, I had envisioned myself as beautiful a boy as Donald or Don. I was sleek and fast on my feet, my fine dark hair falling any which way. As that boy, I had hidden in the roots of trees in the Grunewald, the dark green forest in the heart of Berlin, and walked through it during a thunderstorm that cracked a tree nearby in two. After we moved to Texas and I was almost ten, I was still that boy who could throw a fastball and make it curve, who loved falling to the ground and getting covered with dirt, screw all particulars. My favorite dreams were of me as the cowboy poet, riding my pinto in a roundup and sleeping, my saddle my pillow, under the endlessly inspirational, star-riddled sky. I imagined people, other young girls, falling in love with me, thinking I was really something—fearless, sensitive, with a true heroic air.

After I was given my new identity as a deaf child, all that ardent fancy changed. I fell out of love with my own being, my own body, and lost the sense of myself as the center of my own story. I thought, then, that a hero ought to look like all those beautiful boys whose lives and gender I envied. Meaningfulness seemed somehow interchangeable with the muscular contours of their legs, the tautness of their stomachs. The hair on their arms used to fill me with longing, not just for them but for the love they awoke in my heart. When I stood in front of a mirror, I'd sometimes slap myself silly with disgust. I knew I could never measure up to those tough-looking James Deans with their pouty, kissable lips.

I grew angry at those boys whose lives I envied and could not match. Angry that I'd given them all significance while saving so little for myself, who worked so hard for meaning, as hard as those floating shallow-enders who blew ripples across the surface of the water at Lions Camp. All that anger, envy, and longing fed my craving for stories about the beautiful boys who died. I'd sob with sorrow even as my mind reveled that those bodies, the bodies of the favored, the deeply beloved, were just as treacherous and fragile as the damaged bodies that plagued me and my disabled friends. Every death was a perversely happy reminder that those boys and I shared the same messy inevitability neither they nor I could control.

But Donald's death did me in. It had followed too closely on the heels of Stephen's, which had followed Mark's, which had followed Tim's, which had followed Joe's. By then I didn't want to hear another story about anyone dying, least of all some young man in his prime. I was over my anger, even if I still felt that those boys had been born with a warrant from life that life hadn't given me. It was only as my father was dying that I came to realize I'd given those boys a power that they, like me, had been playing at but never really owned.

About three weeks before my father died in 2006, my sister Tenley noticed that he was pointing the TV remote at the electric wall sockets. When she asked him what he was doing he said, "I'm lining things up." She said, "Daddy, that's a TV remote." He looked at her with pity and replied, "Honey, I've been doing this a long, long time." She said, "You're coming with me. We're going to the hospital." He said, "No I'm not," and sat down in his tweedy, overstuffed La-Z-Boy and wouldn't budge. Tenley went in the kitchen to get Mother, who was on the phone with one of her brothers. "Hang up, Mom," Tenley said. "We've got to get Daddy to the hospital." They headed for a clinic fifteen minutes from the ranchetta and got there in ten. The physicians there took a scan of his brain, thinking perhaps he had fallen. What they saw was a tumor the size of a plum, pressing against his temporal lobe. The physicians told my mother and sister they'd need to transfer him to St. David's in Austin. The local clinic didn't have the equipment to make a full diagnosis. But the minute they showed Mother and Tenley the X-rays, Tenley knew what she was seeing. A neuroglioblastoma. She'd known three other people who'd been given that diagnosis and seen every one of them die.

At St. David's they gave my father steroids to shrink the tumor so he wouldn't be so befuddled, but the steroids made him paranoid and raging. He was sure the Iranian doctor had been sent by terrorists to kill him; that the gay male nurse's aide was trying to poison his water; that after all these years the KGB had finally captured him and were feeding him drugs to torment him with unsettling visions. When my mother tried to explain to him that the hallucinations were from the tumor pressing on his brain, he cut his eyes away and muttered, "That's what *they* say." And when he attacked the nurse's aide with a plastic knife they had him put in restraints.

The first week he was in the hospital, the thing in his head grew to the size of a fist. After the doctors took him off the steroids and he was calm again, they told him and Mother and us that there were no options. There was nothing they could do. He would die. And soon. He refused to listen. They wheeled him into the doctor's office and brought up the image of his brain. "We can't scrape it all out," they told him. "We can get some of it, but a part of it always escapes." He looked at the picture a long, long time. "It's like a bucket of minnows," he finally said. "You put your hand in there and they wiggle away."

Without the surgery, the tumor would probably kill him within a few weeks. He would have seizures. The tumor would grow bigger. There would be more seizures. It would finally take over his brain and he would buck and seize and buck and seize until he finally died. The surgeon said to my mother, "We recommend stopping dialysis. If we do, he will die of kidney failure before the tumor has a chance to kill him." Kidney failure, they said, would be the easier death. He'd simply go to sleep.

As they were bringing him home to die, he showed off his gold wedding band to the ambulance attendants and repeated again and again how much he loved his wife. His first night home, he slept in his own bed and told my mother, "This is the most comfortable mattress in the world." The second day we got him up by saying, "Daddy, you don't need to stay in bed if you can walk." So he got up and proclaimed, "I'm going to walk every single day." And he walked around the circle of trees that marks the driveway—well, walked halfway and then sat on a bench with Mother, looking over the land he'd worked, the house he'd built. They sat there together, holding hands as she sang all the songs they loved from their youth. The next day we made his favorite southern breakfast of biscuits and eggs, ham and grits. That afternoon he said, "I'm going to watch a little TV," and went into the living room, grabbed the remote control, climbed up on the hospital bed, and just didn't want to move. That evening, we tried to feed him, but even the soft food made him gag. He was losing his swallowing reflex. He fell into a light sleep, still clutching the remote, still changing the channels as he dozed. When we tried to take it from his hand, he shook his head and muttered, "I'm putting things in order." Then he began to lapse away.

For the next few days, Mother and Gail would go in the living room every hour or so to sit by his side and sing "Home on the Range," the only song he could ever sing on key, and sometimes he'd sing along with them, in a sweet kind of croaking. We were taking care of his body for him, wiping him, cleaning him, giving him his pain medications by sticking a dropper under his tongue, and when that ceased to work, switched to a suppository. When we'd lift him up, he'd groan and try to turn away. He didn't want anyone but Mother to see him that exposed. But we'd whisper, "It's just us, Daddy. We love you." He never let go of that remote, image following image on the wide-screen TV as his automatic reflex endlessly trolled the ether. Then suddenly it stopped on a NASA channel special about the International Space Station. All that day into the next night, astronauts and cosmonauts floated through their cramped quarters or in the blackness of space, putting things to rights.

He died around four-thirty in the morning a week and a half after he'd been returned to us. We were all asleep but Gail, who had set up camp on the downstairs couch so she could reach out and touch him if he started shivering or shaking. It was Donna who woke me up, and I said, "Oh no, I've got to pee." And did, and then went downstairs to join the others. Mother had gone to the bathroom, too, but to get his dentures, which she handed over to Gail, who, at Mother's insistence, fit them into his mouth, which upset me until I realized he was already gone. Gail said later, "He just took in a breath and never let it go." Gathered there around his body, we broke. We howled like the sad little animals we were. We kissed his hands and cried to the heavens and to him to wake up and be with us again. Our begging seemed never to end. But when it did we sat, spent and exhausted. Then Tenley opened a bottle of wine and we drank it to the dregs.

After that we did what we had done so often when we were all much younger. We fussed over our little father. We dabbed the dried spittle from the lips his mother-in-law had once called "pretty as a girl's." We combed the silvery, baby-fine hair my mother loved to run her fingers though. We washed the thick-muscled torso with its silky covering, the arms so brown and muscular, the hands with their broad palms and clever fingers, the shapely runner's legs, the wide feet with their dancer's arch. And when we removed the sheet to bathe his body entire, before the funeral-home attendants arrived to take him away, we marveled again at what a beautiful boy he had been.

Why I Should Matter

AS A CHILD WHO SUFFERED MIGHTILY from existential doubt, and took enormous pleasure in it, by the way, I grew up thinking that an overwhelming loss of faith in one's existence was an everyday occurrence. But whenever I've mentioned that particular childhood preoccupation to new acquaintances, inexperienced with me or disability, their faces go blank for a second and they take an involuntary step back as if they'd just been introduced to little Wednesday of the Addams Family (*snap! snap!*). My friends with disabilities have reassured me that I'm a not a freak, that when you are born or become imperfect at an early age, meaningfulness isn't something you can ever safely assume. The whole round world can feel like a single eye glaring at your flawed body asking the unanswerable of you in particular—"Why ever should *you* matter?"

Wednesday, that perpetual nine-year-old, would probably just set fire to the questioner, but at her age (and on through the years) I worried that question-as-accusation to a nub. The specter of it sometimes made me so tense I couldn't read children's books that touched on the subject of the thrown-away soul without getting overly emotional. I was a fatalist in my reading. I'd chuck the Whitman hardback the minute Black Beauty's fate seemed to take a turn toward the glue factory, and hiss at the fictional equine-Job trapped in the book on the floor, "Kick someone, bite someone! Just say 'Neigh!'" The deeper into the story I got, the more defeatist I became: "Die, now, horsey. It'll only get worse." I'd read the book a million times but I still didn't trust it to have a happy ending. I felt the same bleak distrust about every other book I read, and the minute conflict was introduced to the plot I'd flip back and forth from that page to the end, just to check, make sure everything came out all right.

At night I'd hug my ratty old teddy bear and sweat out the inscrutable wisdoms I'd soaked up from those books or from the storytelling sessions around the kitchen table. Death was always muscling its way into at least one of the stories, usually by behaving ironically, sneaking up and whacking someone when it shouldn't have and leaving the survivors in a state of spooked uncertainty I found all too familiar. It was Scare on a grand scale, and for all the terror it awoke in me I couldn't help but love the game, love the woe and wonder it awoke in my heart. Those stories about death's capricious ways put me on a more personal, intimate level with the uncaring universe.

Like the story about my Grandpa Chuck running away from home three days past his sixteenth birthday to enlist as a soldier in the war in 1918. He'd snuck away because he knew his mother would come running after and haul him back, so the family had no idea how to get him word of what was happening the years he was gone, how his youngest sister and his father had become sick unto death, not with the flu then sweeping the world in a pandemic but with typhoid fever. For two weeks the father and daughter struggled between life and death, but on the evening of the fifteenth day the young girl took a turn and seemed on her way to recovering. As for the frail old man, the family was sure he would die and die that very night.

The night of that death, Chuck was in an army encampment a thousand miles to the east of his grieving family, sitting on his cot, looking at a snapshot of his three sisters, Marion, Alice, and Edna, when a thought came to him as clear as a voice in his ear: *Who do you choose?* He chose his youngest sister Edna. Instantly. Without quite intending, without knowing the kind of choice he'd made. "And that's why," my mother always adds when she finishes retelling the story, "I got saddled with this damn name," as if that indignity put period to the whole eerie incident. Because, of course, it was the frail old man who lived, and Edna, the younger sister for whom my mother Edna is named, who died.

I used to ponder that little snippet of a story quite a lot. For the mystery of it, yes. But the enigmatic shrouding of that coincidence didn't make my skin prickle as much as the icy thought of my grandfather's after the name Edna popped into his head: *I'd miss her the least.*

The story of Grandpa Chuck's World War I premonition got told quite a lot, and every time it was told, I'd clench the rim of the kitchen table and press my head against it so hard it would make an indentation between my brow and the bridge of my nose that lasted for days. I despised fate for being ironic and just plain mean. Doling out premonitions no one could do a thing about— a young girl, like the infant boy, dying unexpectedly and the ones who were feeling it as it was happening, the ones who could raise the alarm, were just too far removed. I couldn't bear to think of that thought, that wicked voice in my grandfather's head, asking him to choose among his sisters as if he actually had a choice, as if his choice could be anything more than what it was—not just a revelation of whom he knew and loved the least but the punch line of a joke designed to make him look ridiculous. A skinny little sixteen-year-old fearing and believing he had any power whatsoever to effect, when in truth, he was as helpless in his knowing, then, as his mother Eve would be all those years later when she saw the image of a child's coffin in the tea leaves—his own infant son already dead in his crib, the shadow of a future already arrived.

I never ruined a good story with my questions or doubts, but later, at night, I'd flatten myself on my bed and grill the universe. *What's the point of knowing the truth of what's happening,* I'd pressure the void, *when you can't do a damn thing about it?* A good answer was never forthcoming, and I took the silence personally. Because there was that other question lurking around in there, the one I was always facing and always afraid to ask, the question that made me squeeze my teddy bear so hard, the cotton batting in his paws would bulge. *Why does* any *of it matter?* Not just the truth or the way it unfolds, but the lives of all those who have died, will die, are dying now. Me, for instance. Especially me.

I could never find easy answers to that question. Even now, I look for succor from a sense of casual negation, and devour *Reader's Digest* type articles that claim, "You are more important than a quark." I write myself inspirational

Post-its, like the one from grizzled old Mother Teresa, which I remembered and scribbled down as, "Either all life matters or no life matters." After all my earnest effort, it bugs me that I'm still unsettled as to which side of that equation I'm on.

After my friend Laura finished telling me the story about the day she was born—arms foreshortened, flattened flipper-like hands, a bent and twisted lower body, and the attendant physician so taken aback by the deviations of her infant body that he urged her mother to put her aside— I gave her a surreptitious once-over. As we finished up our margaritas I thought, *We all die sometime, but how could that doctor have failed to notice that Laura is as sweet-faced as June Allyson, the long-ago actress who played Jo in one of the early versions of* Little Women? The resemblance was the first thing I remarked on when I met Laura. And I know, because I have held her; her body automatically snuggles when you put your arms around her, just like all the other flirts I've known who were once babies who loved to cuddle. How is it, thinking and knowing all of that, that I still fear what I might have decided if I had been the unknowing mother to whom that doctor whispered his advice?

I only know Laura's story myself because she was part of a writing and performance workshop for people with disabilities in Austin, Texas, called Actual Lives. It was named Actual Lives after the series of workshops I'd been teaching at different universities as a kind of package deal when I was performing one of my solo shows. In the eight years after the PS 122 workshop debacle in England, I kept looking around as I was touring, wondering where all the other cripples were hiding. During all that time, I'd met a mere handful of performers with disabilities and most of them were in a theater group I'd cofounded with Donna Marie in Tallahassee, Florida, the Mickee Faust Club.

The Mickee Faust Club is meant to be North Florida's tongue-in-cheek answer to a certain unctuous rodent living in Orlando, but the name also plays homage to Goethe's good German doctor who, like every single member of the troupe, tussled with the devil of his own desires. Like its central Florida counterpart, the Faust Club is built around a cult of personality. The leader of the club is Mickee Faust himself, the foulmouthed, illegitimate sewer-rat brother of that better-known, better-groomed cartoon creation. In real life, this cigar-chomping, beer-guzzling, hairy-eared, bow-tied rodent is me. Ostensibly, Mickee and his brother Mickey were the only two survivors of their litter—their mother had a salt deficiency she could only satisfy by eating her young. M-I-C-K-E-Y was scooped up by Uncle Walt, and Mickee with two e's was left to tough it out in the gutter.

That's the theatrical conceit of Faust. In reality, it's a self-described "community theater for the weird community." Now, there are many, many weirdos in the wilds of North Florida, and all of them seem to flock to Faust. These weirdos come in a variety of sexual persuasions, a bunch of religions, a range of ages, and with an assortment of disabilities. There is some odd coupling. The ex-Catholic, converted Reform Jew lesbian attorney is close friends with the fundamentalist Christian single mother turned nurses aide to whom God often speaks, but neither has much of a relationship with the Unitarian, transsexual hairdresser and carpenter who had a mild, short-lived flirtation with the straight, male, visually impaired state worker who moonlights nights as a phone-sex worker. But they all get along with the handful of Canadian Mennonites.

The very first weirdo with a disability in Faust (after me) was Maryanne Ward. An imposing woman with a fleshy nose, shrewd dark eyes, and a helmet of salt-and-pepper hair, Maryanne was an opera buff with a nasty wit and a mordant chuckle. As a young woman she'd been a happy contradiction, a true intellectual who lived for the beach. Then the neurofibromatosis kicked in. Tumors began to grow inside her body, almost exclusively along her spine. She had a series of operations to remove or reduce the tumors, but each time her surgeons split her open from neck to waist and scraped them out, the tumors grew right back and with a vengeance. She told me over a glass of wine that when she was first diagnosed, she made a deal with herself: the minute I have to use a cane, she vowed, I'll kill myself; then it was, when I'm in a wheelchair, that's it; then, a power chair will mark the end of it all; until finally she was bedridden and thought, *Oh to hell with the bargaining, I just want to live.* By the time she finally died, she could no longer eat solid foods, or raise her head, or breathe on her own. But she could still laugh and think, and until her last breath, she fought to live.

When she was in Faust, we used her power chair to great effect. It rumbled across the stage as a tank, or glided effortlessly up the ramp during a skit about Egyptian pharaohs; and when Maryanne played one of the fast-food witches in the parody of *Macbeth* she wrote called *McBeef,* she made her chair twirl like Linda Blair's head in *The Exorcist.* I used to envy Maryanne her chair, and if I could have I would have dumped her out of it just to be able to steer it on my own. It had tons of theatrical potential and was always a scene-stealer.

So when I was invited to teach my Actual Lives writing and performance workshop for a semester at the University of Texas in Austin, I thought, *Here's my chance.* For some reason I thought I could attract students with disabilities to my workshops if I simply let it be known that I was deaf. And the odds were good that out of the hordes of students with disabilities who would eagerly line up for my workshop, at least one would have a power chair I could commandeer. Of my thirty-six students that semester, just one was disabled. She had multiple personality disorder. For her final performance project she recorded her different personalities, strapped four different tape recorders to her body, and turned them all on at once. I couldn't hear the particulars but I loved the concept. She got an A.

At the end of the semester, I was bemoaning, over cake and beer with one of the graduate students in the class, my failure to attract students with disabilities to my classroom. Chris, an occupational therapist, was writing her dissertation on autobiography and disability. She had connections to people with disabilities in Austin I didn't. And she knew someone who had access to money to fund a workshop like the one I'd dreamed of doing. She introduced me to Celia, the executive director and money maven of the VSA Arts of Texas—(once known as Very Special Arts, but the organization now goes by the acronym VSA, so as not to use the condescending "special"). I liked them both a lot. They were two disciplined, dedicated women who shared a rowdy streak and a love of good red wine. We three joined forces to become producers of the very first Actual Lives Performance Project, conducted exclusively for people with disabilities.

I had no idea what to expect from the workshop, but except for some interesting digressions, it was pretty much like every other workshop in writing and performance I'd ever done. None of us who were disabled really knew anything about any other disability but our own. But since we were all disabled—with the exceptions of Chris, Celia, and the personal attendants—it became OK to inquire. We spent the first sessions asking each other questions that in mixed company might seem insensitive or rude, the favorite being, "What the hell happened to you?" That spirit of cheerfully uncensored inquiry set the tone for the whole process. We were, after all, in a workshop called Actual Lives, so we might as well examine who we actually were. The only way we were going to find that out was by being blunt about it, poking our noses into each other's business, and asking those leading questions.

I'd learned a few things since that workshop in England. I knew enough not to say, "Take out your pencils and write." Like the PS 122 group, half the people in the Austin workshop didn't have the strength or physical skill to hold a pencil, and some had to struggle cognitively to write at all. But it was simple enough for those of us who could hold a pen to take dictation from the ones who couldn't. Or jot down notes and verbally cue those who had trouble holding on to their thoughts. Or lend our computers to the people who couldn't write in cursive but could type. We were open to any means that got the stories told.

The differences in manual dexterity fascinated me, and it was a treat to watch my friends with cerebral palsy write. My friend Rand's manual dexterity is more broad than refined, and that makes a skill like typing difficult. He prefers longhand. He holds a pencil in his left fist, which he steadies with his right hand, and using both arms he writes his stories on a yellow pad with concentrated if sometimes stabbing slashes, loops, and swirls. The first story he gave me to read was about his days as a freshman at Texas A&M. Rand is on campus his first week, walking around with, as he says, the distinctive cerebral-palsied, gimpy gait, and everyone he sees greets him with a great big "Hi, Al!" All over campus, he's got friends he didn't know he had, all of them saying, "Hi, Al!" One morning he spots another student coming his way who he's never seen before who also has the CP gait. Rand greets him with a shout, "Hey, Al!" This guy spies him and shouts back, "Hey, Rand!" Because that's what everyone on campus had been calling him all those weeks. The mixup might have been more excusable if Rand weren't a tall, slender Anglo, and Al, a short, rotund Mexican American.

We collected a lot of these kinds of stories that we thought were unexpected, funny, or terrible, that made us weep or laugh out loud when they were told. We wanted to put them out there for the community to share, so that's what we did. We translated them in the barest, most rudimentary way for the stage. Just them, the story, and the audience. Even without the bells and whistles, it's never a simple matter to put people who are new to theater onstage. Some people have no idea how to project, where to stand, how to hold for a moment or for a laugh. And for people new to the process who can't project, can't stand, don't perceive the moment or hear the laugh, it's even trickier. The solution, again, was simply to allow ourselves to be curious and ask leading questions. What could all of us in actuality do? And how could we milk it shamelessly, theatrically?

Could the guy with MS steer his power chair at break-neck speed without hurtling over the lip of the stage? What would it take for the blind woman to make her way quickly around the cluttered stage and find her spot? How high could the woman with CP lift her arm, and how long could she hold her finger still so her "Fuck you" would be visible? How easy or difficult would it be for the guy in the manual chair to throw himself out of it and crawl up the stairs to an inaccessible stage? And it's interesting, because, after we began asking ourselves that question, after we started play-ing with our differences and became captivated by them, we started making them part of the script, part of the per-formance itself. There was a twenty-three-year-old woman in the group with advanced juvenile rheumatoid arthritis. She walked with such massive care, shuffling forward inch by careful inch with her cane, that she looked as if she were pushing through a wall of water. In one performance, she paired herself up with four able-bodied dancers whose movements mimicked hers, becoming indistinguishable from them, until the climax of the music when the other four dropped their canes, then whirled and leapt offstage, leaving her behind to make a slow, belabored exit.

I loved those moments of real theater. But what I loved most about the workshops wasn't necessarily the theater created from them. What I loved most were the stories that first arose around the table where we wrote and talked. It felt just like being home again, sitting around the kitchen table as my family told story after story about themselves or people they knew or heard of and all the things that went right or wrong in their lives, talk marked with little displays of how so-and-so yakked a mile a minute or walked with a hitch in their step or died with a snap of the fingers.

The first story Laura told around the table in Actual Lives wasn't the one about her doctor offering to put her aside. It was about growing up everyone's sweetheart. How she loved to cuddle and how her teacher and her friends and her family loved picking her up and cuddling her. They would have carried her around for the rest of her life, if she had let them, taking her anywhere she'd ever dream to go. Now, whenever I feel myself being done in by the same kind of cold, negating eye that once looked upon Laura and saw nothing, I can conjure her stories and look to them for the self-belief that argues for us both. Because that cold stare is still out there, still asking the same old question, which is really a bullying assumption: if a crippled or un-beautiful or queered or female infant isn't deemed worth the effort it might take to keep her alive, then why ever should she persist in her struggle to live?

I still can't answer that question. I can only surround myself with stories that tell me more about who I am and the people I love who are living or have lived in this world with me. Like the stories my mother always tells about the rich snob at her small Texas school, a pasty-faced girl in frills who got the star singing role even though everyone knew my mother had the voice. About almost drowning in a river, and she would have, too, if her Aunt Wee, who was set for church in her silk polka-dotted dress, hadn't seen her go under and, without even kicking off her heels, dove in and pulled my mother up. About going to New Mexico to live with her Aunt Ruby and meeting my daddy, who was a skinny little thing with tons of come-hither in his soft brown eyes. About him trying to get her to go up to his hotel room so he could "'check out his mail,' hah!" About marrying him six weeks later at her parents' house in Texas, and her baby brother Jerry throwing himself against her, crying, "Don't leave us Edna! Don't!" About her father coming out of her brother Kenny's hospital room and saying, moments before the young man was to die, "I think the little guy's gonna make it." About her life in Stuttgart, in Texas, in Berlin. About coming back to the states over a sea so rough the crew had to tie mattresses to the ship's dining room walls. About the dwarf paperman, the one with hooves, who had a crush on her and followed her from Parisian Peyton's, where she worked, into the Woolworth's where she ate her lunch—and how he would click his hooves on the counter in a kind of lovesick code.

Or the tales my sister Tenley tells, looking just like our mother when she tells them, about the various dogs and cats buried in our pet cemetery, like old Oats Eddie, the part beagle, part God knows what, who killed himself by running into the grille of a parked car. Or the gossipy family tidbits Gail loves to reconstruct about the two Eves, those upright, respectable mavens of good cheer and their various ill-fated romances. Aunty Eve and her three husbands—the wastrel she divorced, the milquetoast nobody remembers, and the handsome wildcatter who was squashed to a pulp by a toppled oil rig the very day Aunty boarded the train in Philadelphia to travel cross-country to join him in Oklahoma City. Or the secret of Great-Grandma Eve's child by her hush-hush first marriage and how, not long after that divorce, her ex showed up on horseback outside the out-of-the-way, two-room shack in rural Pennsylvania where she and her child had fled. There were a dozen members of the Klan riding with him. He broke his way into the house, pulled his daughter out of her mother's arms, and when Great-Grandma Eve followed him out the door, clawing and screaming, he spread his hand over her face and forced her down into the mud, then kicked her in the kidney. At his signal, the Klan threw their torches onto the cabin roof, and then, as the hut went up in flames, they all rode off into the coming dawn, he with the child tucked under his arm like a package. Eve was left alone, shivering in her nightgown, muddied from head to toe, nothing to be salvaged from the ashes. Years later, that child showed up at her mother's doorstep. No one but Eve's second husband and her sister—not even her son, Chuck, or her three daughters, Marion, Alice, and Edna—having ever known about that terrible first marriage; and the child a ringer for her father right down to his foul mouth and talent at cards. After a week of Eve's house rules, the girl got bored and disappeared again only to reappear decades later, looking like an elderly floozy, to weep and wail and throw herself across her mother's coffin, much to the dismay of her half brother and two surviving half sisters, who'd done their own quiet grieving in private.

Or the story Alice—a striking, former Texas deb and my close friend since our days performing together at both Winedale and Esther's—told me about her older brother David, who had CP much more severe than Rand's. And if he couldn't walk or feed himself, he was a sociable boy who loved to talk, even if his speech was clear only to those who knew him well. His hands were too spastic to hold anything like a pencil or a brush, so he used his feet to write and paint. He loved a good book and graduated from high school with top grades, went on to take some college courses, and had a genuine wit. He was a blond-haired, blue-eyed boy, as handsome as his sister Alice was beautiful. When he came of age, his yearning to be made whole led him—despite the objections of his family—to opt for an experimental operation touted by a preeminent surgeon of the day. The operation was simple enough. The surgeon drilled two tiny holes through the right and left sides of David's skull, then pumped them full of pure grain alcohol. The doctor was testing his own private theory that the pressure of the alcohol would create a bubble that might somehow relieve the part of the brain that controlled David's gross motor skills. All it really did was give David the fever that cooked his brain. That sweet boy lingered for a year after the operation, but he died despondent and was never able to speak another word.

Or the story my sisters and I love to tell our friends about the last week of our father's life, which Tenley has taken to calling "The Miracle of the Ponds." My father, Paul, was the last boy and second-to-last child in the second family of John Calvin Galloway, a sometime farmer and roving Baptist minister from Reeltown, Alabama. John Calvin outlived his first wife, whose name is unknown to me—probably breeded her to death, because he already had thirteen children full grown when he married my father's mother, Jesse Ida May Virgina Jones, a spinster graduate of Teacher's College and a woman who always had her nose in a book. Jesse May gave birth to nine children in as many years. My father loved his mother but remembered her as a screamer—always shouting at her numerous children to finish their chores. The only time she wasn't screaming was late at night when the children were supposedly abed and she could read in peace by lantern light. My father, a dark-eyed, tenderhearted boy, was the pet of his large family. After Jesse May was widowed, the local doctor pressured her to give my father to him for adoption. "Your son, " he told her, "has too good a mind. It oughtn't be wasted on the hardscrabble life you and yours live." She threw a book at the good doctor and her older three boys ran him off the property.

My father was working as a janitor to put himself through college when World War II began. He enlisted first as a glider and helicopter pilot/mechanic. But the day after one of the then-experimental helicopters dropped from the sky and burst into flames that engulfed the pilot, his best friend Rippendale, he resigned from the air force and signed up for army language school. There he found out he had a knack for accents—that he could imitate the precise inflections not just of people living in a particular region in Germany but of inhabitants of individual towns within that region. That's how my father came to be an operative for the Counter Intelligence Corps in postwar Germany. He was a successful operative but he had a streak of the wild. A liberal in a conservative profession, he often found himself stationed in out-of-the-way places like Alaska. After he started working with the Office of Economic Opportunity, he grew even more liberal. The day Nixon decreed that all federal workers had to be clean-shaven, my father promptly grew a beard. When finally Nixon's shit-ass policies drove my father from the job he loved, Daddy retired to the piece of land he'd been cultivating in central Texas, a peaceful, pretty little place shaded by a cluster of oaks. There he built by hand the two-story stone and wood house where he died and where my mother still lives.

He was a funny, gentle man, who loved quoting the comic strips, composing slightly dirty limericks, and telling us all the new jokes he'd heard, but he never talked directly about the things he had seen and done when he was who he was during the Cold War. Whenever we girls would start to pester him with questions about that part of his life, his face would go tight and blank, as if to warn us off the subject. "I could tell you things," he once said, "you really wouldn't want to know." And that would be that. After he died my mother read through all six volumes of his diary. But they held only numbers—the number of miles he'd run on a particular day, the time he'd started, the hours it had taken him. Occasionally she'd find among the numbers a line like, "The dog died today. Ran eight more miles."

Texas was in the middle of a drought the August our father was diagnosed with the neuroglioblastoma that would kill him. There are two big ponds on our Texas property and both of them had gone bone-dry. My little sister Tenley had been wishing/praying (although we are not the praying type) that there would be a rain that would fill the ponds up one last time for our dad to see. A few days before our father died, we had visitors—Donna Marie's oldest brother, Michael, and his wife, Eileen. When Michael came into the house, he remarked that our ponds were full. We all screamed "What!" and ran out to see, and yes indeed, they were brimming.

We didn't really yet have time to marvel. We were afraid that it was a leak in our water pipes that had filled them. So we called the Chisholm Trail water company to ask them, and they said Well, if there's a leak it's yours, because we are a huge, efficient company and we don't have leaks. So we thought fuck them and called a plumber who looked for a leak on our end of things and couldn't find one but fixed the broken downstairs toilet instead. Then he and Tenley went down to the water meter by the creek to check and see if there was a leak there. And lo and behold there was. The huge Chisholm Trail water main had busted and was filling our ponds to the brim to the tune of several thousands of gallons of water.

So we told our dad, who was still up and walking. And he looked out at the water and laughed, then got on the phone and called the Chisholm company and kind of rubbed it in by thanking them for filling up our ponds at their expense. And while he was on the phone he told them, too, that he was dying, or that's what his doctors said but he himself was skeptical although he'd know by the end of the week because that's all the time they gave him to live.

A handful of days later, at midnight, Tenley drove to the Conoco station, where Daddy used to buy his scratch-off lottery cards, to pick up a gallon of milk. The young Iranian clerk who always swapped jokes with Daddy asked how he was doing. Tenley told him that Daddy had died two days before. The clerk cried when he first heard the news, Tenley said. But when she told him the story about the ponds, he whispered, with the most faithful expression of belief in his eyes, "It's a miracle!" And so we all agreed that maybe it was.

I like stories with hokey, happy endings almost as much as those that end in a thud—like the only story my father ever bothered to tell us girls about his own father, John Calvin, that good-natured itinerant Baptist minister who one day seemed to go crazy, never violent, but he was seeing things that weren't there and causing enough commotion about what he saw to bring the local sheriff to their home. When the sheriff got out of his car to take him away, Jesse Ida, John Calvin's young second wife, pregnant then with their ninth child, ran into the house, got a gun out of her kitchen drawer, and went back out to shoot the law and would have, too, if her eldest son hadn't stuck his hand between the hammer and the trigger. The sheriff cuffed John Calvin and took him off to a mental institution in Tuskegee, just thirty miles from his home, but in those days it might as well have been a million. There he died without ever seeing his family again. Only after his death did they discover he had pellagra, a vitamin deficiency that was then a scourge of the southern poor.

If I don't matter, neither does that poor southern man. Nor does his son who was my father. Neither does the young Texan named Edna who died of typhoid nor the lush little beauty Edna for whom she was named. Nor does the fragile baby Robert who died in his crib or the two identical Eves who loved and held him. Nor do those two beautiful boys, both named Donald, both so thin when they died the needles went right through them.

If they don't matter then neither does anyone else whose name I've evoked in this small book I've written, including Shakespeare, Mother Teresa, June Allyson, and FDR. And while I may have trouble believing in the meaningfulness of my own life, I have a little less trouble believing in the meaningfulness of theirs. In every sentence, every word of stories told I feel the presence of something still unspoken or as yet unheard, and I feel it as an emptiness akin to hope. There are so many more of us out here who don't know how to tell our own stories or make our own small triumphs compelling or simply convince others that we have souls as complex (or perhaps more so) as any movie star, politico, or prince of the realm. If we don't or won't or simply can't tell our own stories, does that mean we matter less or not at all?

When I'm at a loss to answer that question, it helps me to summon up the memory of my wicked other, the small, dense, shadowy *them* I glimpsed trapped in the netherworld I visited when I was nine. I like to imagine it fuming in there, thwarted in its self-serving nasty scheme to possess my body for its own frenzied use. I imagine it pissed and spitting, so set on living, it would still try and race me to the source. I just know that if anyone were to question its own mean little right to live, it would hiss at them, like a terrorist: "If I don't matter, then neither do you. Neither does anything or anyone. Nor does life itself." I'd have no trouble at all reading its lips.

A Happy Life...

THERE IS NO PLACE for sentiment in the world of disability. It demands a toughness of mind and being I've never quite had. I've cried over my deafness and my inability to handle the cards I was dealt. I've fallen into depressions for which I have been hospitalized. At times, I abused drugs and liquor. I've flown into jealous rages and resented my friends who had become successful or moneyed or simply happy in their lives, and attributed their success solely to the keenness of their ears. I still remain, at fifty-seven, excessively critical of professional theater I'm not in and still blame my exclusion from it on my lateral lisp or the visibility of my hearing aids. Not even the beauty of nature gives me peace, because nature, with its zebra-stalking lions, smirking hyenas, and cannibal chimps, is a constant source of worry. It has never been lost on me that if I were reduced to my natural state I'd be nature's dinner de jour. Contrary to many of my deaf and disabled peers, I think the particularities of my deafness are disabling, that disability itself isn't a badge of honor any more than it's a curse

of the gods, and that the cure for what ails me is not geno-
cide, and I want to be cured.

So I'm grateful that I'm no longer as deaf as I once was,
that technology has caught up with me. For most of the
years of my deaf life I wore standard analog, welfare hearing aids that gave me a crude illusion of sound—they let
me know that a truck or a thunderstorm might be bearing
down, but that's as subtle as they got. I grew up satisfied
with that, thinking, even as a child, that I was long past
the age of miracles. Then came microchips, computers,
and the digital hearing aids that threw my hushed life into
clamorous turmoil.

I was forty years old when I was fitted with my first digital hearing aids, but my audiologist said, right before she
opened the door, "Give me your hand." I raised an eyebrow
but did as she said. Then she opened the door and it was
like the doctor opening the French windows for my dying
mother. A pulse starting up again, the empty world newly
aroar. The whirring of engines, the whoosh of a breeze,
the clattering clanging of God knew what, and the voice
by my ear telling me something I couldn't understand but,
miracle of miracles, could hear and knew from the tone to
be reassurance. I broke into a sweat and plastered myself
against the opened door, clutching her hand to my chest as
if it were a cross and I had just seen the face of the Virgin
Mary on a grilled cheese sandwich.

The sounds seemed like an invisible weight pressur-
ing me to a standstill. When finally I was able to move, I
told my audiologist I loved her, said goodbye, startled by
the loudness of my own voice, then rushed to my car and
slammed the door, which made me yelp. When I started
the car, I thought the power of it would rip my head off

my shoulders. I turned the radio on and it was nothing but jibber but at least it was jibbering, something it had never done before. My brain was a tilt-a-whirl frantically trying to sort though the noises assaulting it. Finally I gave up, took the digitals off, and retreated into happy silence. Back home I put them on again and discovered something Donna Marie had long alluded to, that our quiet little house was actually on a main thruway. Cars and trucks and motorcycles squealing and grinding past at all hours. I was hearing all the hard, heavy sounds and a few of the lighter, funnier ones, like rain rattling against a tin roof like a woodpecker with the shakes. Still no trilling birds, no crickets chirping, no trickling springs, no whispered words of love, but the world more alive for all that. It took days before I could wear those new hearing aids for any length of time, weeks before my brain stopped jumping and shivering at every new clatter and shout, and months before it settled down to relearn lost sounds. One afternoon I was out walking on the dirt path of a tree-canopied park near our little cottage, when my brain suddenly realized I was hearing a deep, long yowling; it took another few seconds for my brain to sort through itself and identify that yowling as the whistle of a train making its way over a bridge not a yard from where I stood. Until that moment I hadn't realized the bridge existed.

As a toddler I had known the fullness of sound, and through the decades I remembered that feeling and never stopped yearning for its return. As a young woman I used to take off my hearing aids and lie in bed at night surrounded by my fate and wonder, *What is this? Foul subtraction or blessing in disguise?* Even then the answer was complex, because there was, I had to admit, a kind of peace in the silence, albeit an uneasy one. But from the day I realized I was going deaf, sound became my lost love. And here, in part, it was again. Having it return threw me into a depression so deep Donna Marie feared I might never recover. I couldn't get over how easily it could be fixed, this slipup that had caused me lifelong struggle and grief and took away what I always secretly thought was my rightful life.

In that life I'd be someone who hates clichés instead of the dolt who adores them. Clichés are so easy to lip-read. I see the lips take a certain shape and know exactly the phrase coming and that puts me one satisfying step ahead of the conversation. In my twilight-zone parallel universe, I'd not only be blisteringly original in conversation, I'd have (I'm convinced, contrary to the opinion of everyone else in my family) a voice like my mother's, a deep, growly, bluesy purr loaded with sex and an excess of feeling. That would have been mine, I just know it. A true indestructible talent that would have given me my meaningfulness wrapped up in a bow.

I'm convinced, too, that I'd be earning a steady living doing animated voice-overs. Porky Pig, Daffy Duck, the wheezy cop, the gum-smacking moll. During my earliest childhood I could turn down the TV volume and launch into perfect imitations of the stuttering oinker, the spluttering canard, the ain't-no-dumbbell blonde. To this day, I can still, as they say, do the police in different voices, if only those voices I once heard as a child.

Or maybe it would have given me the independence to strike out looking for a life of my own making, instead of one that has always felt compromised by my own insecurity. What adventurer can strike off across the icy tundra when they're worried about getting hearing aids wet? I became overly cautious when I went deaf, and for good reason. Bad things often announce themselves ahead of time with a screech or a boom or an ominous cracking or a nasty chuckle. Sometimes when I'm walking by myself at night, without even quite knowing that I'm doing it, I stop, narrow my eyes, and look this way and that, as if I've come to a dangerously trafficked intersection, quiet at the moment but subject to speedy change.

After I was fitted with digitals and that little bit more of hearing was returned to me, I convinced myself that if I could have heard that way all along I'd have been me a hundred times better. A me who wouldn't keep trying to write and speak in easily inflected iambic pentameter; who could churn out page after page of actually remembered, if cleverly reconstituted, dialogue. Hearing would have added two inches to my height, slimmed my thighs, and given me much-needed fashion sense, letting me grow up into the sunny little devil I was meant to be instead of some morose ingrate brooding over the tragedy of a sense only partially restored.

I got over that exercise in extreme self-indulgence the day I was offered a cochlear implant that would restore the rest of my lost hearing. I didn't want it. I took one look at the surgical diagram and said, "You'll have to kill me first." Which wasn't the reaction the doctor had hoped for. They didn't know my history as a childhood freak, weighted down by what seemed like tons of hardware and gadgetry. The cochlear-implant aid was the size of a fist. It would button to my head. I'd lose whatever residual hearing I had. And from then on voices would have a distinct robotic quality. No, I said. Absolutely not. I'm too old, too vain, and I don't want something that buttons to my head.

I fled the office the same way I'd once fled the Museum of Natural History, only it wasn't the specter of the end of the world pursuing me. Or maybe it was.

Just like that, I don't need to be deaf. Poof! Cured of my defining curse. And that unsettles me. So much of my identity hangs on being little-*d* deaf. It is how I have defined and measured myself all my life. Without my deafness, who will I be?

I'm about to find out. Recently, when I was giving a friend a quick rundown on the evils of cochlear implants, I happened to glimpse my reflection in the window of the cafe where we were having our coffee and chat. What I saw reflected there looked like a snarly, neo-Luddite quacking Daffy Duck. I had to laugh. I just looked so wrong. I decided maybe I'd better give things a little more thought. So I thought about my initial resistance to that first change from analog to digital. Remembered how like a miracle it seemed when the neighbor's good little dog started barking its fucking head off and the heretofore silent phone started ringing every ten damn minutes. I remembered, too, my own father, seldom without a book in hand, whose complications from diabetes frayed the lacy tissues of his retina until he could no longer read. And how for long months he sat in a stoic daze not sure what to do with himself without his morning paper, his westerns, or his *Alfred Hitchcock's Mystery Magazine*s. We finally persuaded him to go with us to a store that sold the seeing aids he claimed he didn't need. He stood just inside the doorway until the salesman turned on one of the magnifiers—a huge machine designed to adjust the size of the print and the level of light so that even the legally blind could read. The light caught my father's eye. He stepped toward it, sat down at the machine, read the first line of text, then settled in to read the whole boring brochure. He might as well have whooped.

I have to keep remembering that technology gave my father back so much of what he lost, reintroduced me to a forgotten part of myself that I loved; that all around me now the world is filled with sounds that still elude me, most of them, my family and friends tell me, annoying. But I'll take them all as is. I'm opting for the cochlear implant.

There's a qualifier. I'm going to wait a year or two longer until the technology improves. I still don't want a button on my head. I still don't want anything more visible than my hearing aids already are. I want nanotechnology to produce a bionic ear that will fit invisibly inside my real one and create sounds in my brain that exactly mimic the sounds I'd perceive if I could really hear. Years ago that would seem too much to ask for, but now those tools are almost made.

I will always be caught up in a tangle of resentment at the accident that befell me even before I was born, but the morning after I decided I would, indeed, get the implant, I awoke in a sleepy muse. As I lay there, I imagined the world of science already up and abuzz. Somewhere someone in a white lab coat was tinkering, maybe using a microscope and tweezers to piece together a cochlear device the size of a Barbie doll's foot. And soon, oh soon, that intricate machine would be ready to be tucked unobtrusively away inside the tunnel of my ear. Like gay marriage in the Deep South, there seemed a jolly inevitability to it all. I felt sure both those miracles would soon enough be visited upon me. In the meantime, I clicked on my already obsolete new digitals and a sudden, thundering whoosh told me that Donna Marie was up taking a shower, a chuffing by my ear let me know that Tweety, the dainty black cat with emerald eyes and a tail like a feathered boa, wanted breakfast and then out. That morning, the little bit more I'd been given to hear no longer felt like delayed and bitter restitution, but like the gift and promise that it was. Lying abed surrounded by that cozy domesticity of sound—the shower, the cat, the book falling off the bed onto the floor, my own deep, grunting sigh—it seemed churlish not to admit that mine was a happy life, when I could stand it.

ACKNOWLEDGMENTS

I have a large extended family, the Cunninghams and the Galloways, which includes my nephews, Paul Adams and Michael Parr, Michael's wife, Jennifer, and his father, Bill; and now, too, the Nudd clan into which I married: all whom I love and with whom my life and memories are intertwined. I also have another family of whom that is true—my dear friends over the years. Some are mentioned by name in this very selective recollection of my life and some are not, but they are all a part of that web of remembrance.

This book has had many readers to whom I owe thanks, including Alice Gordon, Beatrice Queral, Susan Gage, Carol Batker, Carrie Sandahl, Del Poey, Ernie Sharpe, and Stan Kern. Isabelle Potts, Jill Dolan, and Rand Metcalfe gave it their particular attention, as did Cheri Ward and Jayme Harpring, who, when the book was derailing, helped me edit it back on track. And thanks, too, to Martha Vicinus for inspiring the perfect closing line.

My most constant readers have been my mother, Edna, my two sisters, Gail (Trudy) and Tenley, and, when he lived, my sweet father, Paul. We had hundreds of lively family debates about whose story was the right one, or at least the most entertaining. The most entertaining stories in this book were taken right out of their mouths. But aside from my faithful agent, Colleen Mohyde, who read every paragraph I sent her over the years, the most devoted and critical audience for this memoir has been Donna Marie Nudd.

I also want to thank everyone at Beacon Press, including managing editor Lisa Sacks and copyeditor Melissa Dobson, and especially my two exceptionally keen and observant editors, Joanna Green and Gayatri Patnaik. They love books at Beacon and are good to the people who write them.

Thanks, everyone! I loved writing this memoir, even when it was tearing me apart.

AFTERWORD

Reader, I did it. I got the cochlear implant. Not quite against my will, but far sooner than I'd thought.

I'd been content with my two digital hearing aids, fancying them the technological be-all and end-all, able to eke sounds out of dead air. The audiologist who fit me with those two assured me they were among the most powerful aids known to mankind. "When you switch them on," she said, "it's like flipping the switch to a space shuttle."

Hearing aids that powerful are delicate, usually last a handful of years, and cost the earth—about three grand apiece. So I was unnerved when the two of them simultaneously went belly-up. I'd been mulling implants but imagining I had another half decade of stalling before I'd need to give them a second thought. The future was suddenly right here.

I'd been offered implants twice before, and each time I had issued a curt, snake-eyed refusal: The first time because the technology was crude—a fat little box on top of my head. Too like the long-ago fat little box between my boobs. The second time because I just didn't want to. I'd made peace with my deafness, written a solo show and this memoir about it. I had deafness figured out. I couldn't imagine how a cochlear could make any more difference than a NASA-grade hearing aid. I wanted to hold out for some science fictiony nanotechnology that would basically regrow my inner ear.

And then the aids went wonky. I needed a solution that wasn't my trusty masking tape. But any solution was going to require money I didn't have. This was the not-so-long-ago days when Donna Marie and I were kept by law from marrying. Not only were Donna and I gay in America; we were gay in Florida, where queers are still hunted like grouse. That boils down to no shared health insurance. And like most deaf/disabled lesbian performance artists, I was, uh, underemployed at the time. Money was scarce.

Social services it was. I thought I'd try my usual trick of performing "disabled," but the world had progressed somewhat. My assigned counselor had exactly the same kind of deafness I did and saw right through the act. As it turned out Robyn, my counselor, was queer herself. (We *are* everywhere.) And Robyn had once used the small kind of mini shuttle hearing aids I had, and she was pushing hard for me to do as she had done and get a cochlear implant. I remained unimpressed by her arguments until in the middle of our conversation she reached over, rummaged in her purse, picked up her cell phone, and took a call. I was overcome by the white-hot flame of cell phone envy, which is way worse than penis envy because everyone has a cell phone.

I mention in this memoir a clever little machine that allowed me to make phone calls: the TTY. A wonderful innovation at the start, but after years of using it I came to regard it as the TD-ious. I will spare you the details of its use, but believe me, in comparison, nothing seemed sexier than the ease with which Robyn picked up her phone. I still wasn't sold. But I was intrigued.

Later that evening, Donna, after being told about Robyn and her cell phone, and well knowing my simmering resentment of the TTY, said, "Terry, why should you have to work so hard? Get the implants."

Before I could get anywhere near the implants, I had to first prove that I was indeed deaf and hadn't been faking it all these decades to reap the glamorous benefits of social services. I was ushered into a soundproof room and told to sit down, jack up my jerry-rigged digital hearing aids, and listen to a recording of a man saying fifty-two common sentences. I was to repeat each sentence exactly as I heard it. I thought, *Hmmm, well, I can hear so much better with these little digital suckers, wonky as they are. I'm gonna ace this.*

Out of those fifty-two sentences I got a single word right: "the." And that was a wild guess.

They ushered me into a second room where the audiologist, who was really cute, sat across the table from me. As I eyed her lips with deaf, lesbian avidity, she parroted those same fifty-two sentences. I got fifty-one of the fifty-two sentences correct. I thought that fifty-second sentence was just a word: "Israeli." But I remembered in the nick of time that it was sentences I was supposed to be repeating and immediately corrected myself: "It's raining." Lip-reading skill: 99 percent! Hearing skills: pfffffttt.

I was deaf enough all right.

I actually thought and was telling everyone I was having brain surgery because, you know, drama. It's not. The surgeon makes a cut behind the ear, slits open the mastoid bone, and implants tiny electrodes directly into the cochlea. Using his forefinger, he then tucks an internal processor into the pocket he's made between the muscle and bone. Your ear is dead for the month it takes to heal. But once you've mended, you are ready to go "hot," cochlear vernacular for switching the interior processor on. It tickles me to use the word as if it were the sexiest act in the world. Donna came with me on my own sizzling day of reckoning.

Katherine Gray was the calmly beautiful audiologist who was set to guide me back to the land of the hearing. Katherine ushered Donna and me into a quiet room where she placed the $75,000 supercomputer over my ear and attached it to the magnetic processor inside my head. Donna held my left hand; Katherine, my right. Then Katherine switched on the marvelously intricate machine that would give me back to the world I had lost.

And I wanted to rip my fucking head off.

My brain had tilted and whirled when I'd first tried digital hearing aids, so I thought I knew what was coming before Katherine flipped that switched.

Hah.

That quiet room exploded into the cacophonous blast of every sound in the world. This time my body didn't bother to sweat; it turned icy white and cold. The commotion going on in my brain made the hubbub stirred up in there by the digital aids seem like a flick of a finger. The room lifted up and set itself back down. My stomach dropped. I tore away from the hands that held me, covered my eyes, and cried, "Oh, no, I can't do this, Donna! I can't do this!"

When we had first entered that room I'd noticed an array of sound makers scattered across the table. One of those was an old-fashioned hotel bell. In the middle of my panting terror, Katherine leaned over and hit that bell with the flat of her hand. It rang with a single, clear, echoing note, and, as if summoned, my entire being turned and fastened on that sound. So beautiful. So pure. And I was hearing it.

From that moment, I was in love.

But the isle, as Caliban says, is full of noises, and I had only the vaguest idea of what they were. This new state of hearing was so different from my previous years of deafness, I was having to relearn yet again what it meant to hear. Surprisingly, it's not something the brain automatically knows how to do.

Those fast, repetitive ticking noises? A clock? Rain on a tin roof? Computer keys? Stiletto heels? The sound that felt like blood rushing through my ears, was it indeed blood rushing through my ears or was it the air conditioner? And that horrible robotic screeching? Was that coming from Donna's mouth?

It was coming from Donna's mouth.

In the beginning, all voices sounded like R2-D2's, and the brain takes its own sweet time to translate them from "SOUOOMMING LAHK AHHHISS" to "something like this."

The audiologist tells you that the process of learning is confusing, frightening even. But you have to keep at it, keep listening to everything. Keep the radio on, the TV on; don't look at the captions. Listen. I kept the car radio on constantly. The progress is like climate change: slow, slow, slow, and then inevitable and breathtakingly swift. One afternoon, as I was making a left-hand turn, my brain amazed me by shifting into focus and plunking me right in the middle of an NPR discussion about Bridezillas.

Not much later I went home to hear my mother's voice

for the first time since I was nine. She came running out to the car and cried, "Terry, kin ya heer me?" "Mom," I said, dumbfounded, "you've got a Texas accent!"

The first change I noticed in the world were the birds. I had known they existed. I'd seen them flying hither and thither, but I didn't have any inkling of how ubiquitous they were. Birds, birds everywhere. Now I could see them in the trees, drawn there by their cries. And they didn't just tweet but made lots of scary noises. Screeching, cawing, shrilling. Hitchcock was right: they're conspiring to kill us.

The first change people noticed in me was my speech—how crisp it was becoming, how clear. I had struggled and worked for years to keep my speech from losing vowels and smudging consonants. But I couldn't hear how my tongue wasn't quiet hitting my palate. I simply could not perceive what was missing, what my body was doing wrong. And now, no sweat—my brain was effortlessly perceiving and correcting my mistakes.

Over time the miracle has settled in.

I can pick up my sexy cell phone and call anyone I want, even if I now usually just text. I rest easy tracking our little cat's whereabouts by the tinkling of the bell on her collar. I hear our refrigerator humming its grumbling paean to its own bountifulness and it makes me feel cheery. And now when I'm driving with my family late at night, sitting in the backseat dozing off, I hear again their comforting murmur. All that was lost has been regained.

I'm cured, right? The cure I've spent my entire life being suspicious and scornful of has been visited upon me, leaving me elated. And sick with guilt.

Because there is another change brewing. I'm forgetting. Forgetting what it meant to be deaf. Forgetting the lost intimacies when Donna didn't dare lean in to whisper sweet nothings in my ear, because my hearing aids would scream bloody feedback murder.

Forgetting how I'd gone to movies, plays, performances, or poetry readings and sat there in a blank-faced stupor because nothing was captioned and I couldn't read lips from afar well enough to tell where the language was taking me.

Forgetting how unforgiving and mean the world felt when I couldn't keep up, through no fault of my own, no matter how hard I swam. Forgetting how mean the world can still be to my friends who can't be cured or don't want curing.

Forgetting how I used to laugh with my crip friends over the fixation the Able Bodied have on the Cure, how we used to bitch that people who didn't know us couldn't believe we are anything more than our disabilities. We could have odd hobbies, sexual quirks, pet peeves, part-time jobs, and wayward children, but to Them we were still just the deaf girl, or the blind guy, or the whatever that is in the wheelchair. They wanted us cured so badly they'd beg us to let them pray over our bodies. My Granny Doris was a case in point. But that was not a personal and isolated incident. Every one of my disabled camarados has a similar story.

I mentioned my buddy and neighbor Rand earlier in this memoir. He of the cerebral palsy that gives him what he calls his gimpy-guy gait. Rand loves to tell the story about how he was out mowing his lawn one Sunday when a white van drove by his house, stopped, then reversed. A group dressed in their Sunday best got out and trooped over to where he was mowing. The leader said, "God did

not mean for you to be this way. May we pray over you?"
Rand thought it over a second, decided it couldn't hurt,
and said OK. As a group, they put their hands on his head,
shoulders, and arms and started praying. And they prayed.
And they prayed. Rand was getting tired of the joke and
wanted lunch. So he threw himself flat on the ground and
shouted, "What the hell did you do to me? I can't move!"

Rand and I laugh about how deft and funny he is at de-
flecting unctuous attention, how we both resist becoming
inspirational cripples, the ones who inspire gasps of awe for
our bravery in simply existing. Or worse, the ones freed by
the miracles of science and technology to say bye-bye to all
that and slip away from their disabled histories like snakes
shedding skin. Now suddenly I feel in danger of becoming
one of the worse. So enamored with my own cure, I've become oblivious, wandering off to leave my friends to fend
for themselves. A fucking traitor, claiming it's no longer
my fight—this particular messy struggle for meaning, to
matter, be heard, be worthy of life. And because my body
is no longer urgently calling me to remember, forgetting.

I could plead helplessness because I remain besotted
with this new sense of mine. Windshield wipers that swish
in the rain or pull squealing rubber against dry glass. Doors
that creak. You can hear yourself pee! Who knew? Crickets that drive you crazy, and the wind really does blow
through the trees as if it's talking to you or just making a
racket. I am in love still and forever after with the noises of
living, the world's buzzing confusion.

So I promise myself I will lose nothing from this miracle. The things I've always fought for are still my fight and
one I needn't worry about forgetting. All I have to do to
remind myself is walk across the street and talk with Rand.